PRAISE I

Spiced by so ... ironic wit, lucid ... sounds, tastes and smells; an experience close to riding on the journey; war-torn areas, land mines; societies in political turmoil, corruption; seething ethnic conflicts barely attenuated. Yet, Mansfield finds beauty, freedom and fellowship within the chaos.

Jim Cowgill, ADVMoto

I loved it, one of the best written books I've read; humorous, adventurous, informative. Exquisite writing, amazing.

Nathan Millward. The Postie

I learned, laughed, sympathised and was surprised. It's very easy to give five stars.

Sam Manicom, Under Asian Skies

Just occasionally a book arrives that is different, brave and definitely intriguing; an observational classic, the acerbic wit pin sharp.

Paddy Tyson. Overland Magazine

A refreshing, sometimes unnervingly different approach; a 'why-you-should-do-it' inspirational book.

Colin Overland, Ride Magazine

I

NFTR8.5

NOTES FROM THE ROAD
VOLUME III

Mark

DEREK MANSFIELD

Adventure begins when you step through the door!

Derek Mansfield

Hombre Press
First published by Hombre Press
England, September 2017

First Printing, 2017

ISBN 978-0-9957454-9-0

Edited by Several People
Designed by Olga Popova
Printed by Zenith Media

VERITAS ME DIRIGIT

TRUTH DIRECTS ME

Here's a truth that I've discovered.

When you've seen sufficient oceans, and marvelled at the mountains, when you've walked the city streets and ridden enough of the steppe… it's the people you meet that are the most remembered.

They're the reason for the journey.

DEDICATION

This book is dedicated to my grandchildren, Luke & Rosabella.

May they grow ever more clever and strong and explore this wonderful world for themselves.

CONTENTS

FOREWORD

I am lucky to have completed this book.

I have three illnesses, any one of which is terminal, but I'm still upright and breathing today.

Certain names, places and times have been changed to protect people from consequential retribution as they helped me on my journey.

Gangsters are woven into the story and they still live. Others, friends, were involved in small but illegal acts against some Nation States

But I made it there, and I made it back.

Thank you for the love, each and every one of you.

PROLOGUE

The much-feared Buran wind stirs into life in the north of Siberia, gathers pace on the Mongolian Steppe, and crashes into Kazakhstan. In winter, it is ice laden. In summer, in the now, on broken roads, it whips sand and soil into deadly dust storms.

Because I have no choice I ride half blinded over a hill; a burly SUV overtakes and throws more dust into my eyes. The deep sand is not gentle with the front wheel under full brake.

To the road bed, pain shooting through my body from ribs broken five weeks earlier. Breathing is stilted; a few short gasps and new pain blossoms from my ankle trapped under a quarter tonne of motorcycle.

I turn my head and see the wheels of a giant Kamaz truck sliding towards me. "Dear God," I beg, "beam me up."

1

And Off

It's the drugs that take up the space.

There was a time, employed as I was as an ambassador of an august international newspaper, coloured pink, when I was provided with an expense account with which to entertain clients.

The entertainment was supposedly to persuade the clients to spend their corporate funds on advertising in said organ. Many of the advertisers were bankers in the City of London.

Some of the more corpulent entertainees actually and audibly smacked their lips over food and wine thus freely provided, and told stories that the hills in the vineyard that made this wine faced south, or north or somewhere, therefore improving the wine beyond human capacity of description, adjectives or judgement. Thick lips, smack smack, guzzle guzzle, glug glug.

I never heard a geographic or geological discussion over the merits of marijuana or cocaine or other recreational drugs. But then I may not have been listening; I lived for a couple of decades with more than my share of blackouts.

No matter the provenance, my sole interest in fine or any kind of wine, alcohol or other recreational stimuli was always the same. More. Now.

But personally, no lips were smacked.

Drugs needed for recreation can be purchased almost anywhere on the road; but the maximum allowable prescribed drugs needed to keep me alive for four months take up a great deal of room. In the days of the brown glass bottle it was much easier to pack, but today the pills are divided by paper, card and plastic the easier to forget and administer in the wrong order. Or time.

I'd packed most things two days ago. Clothes, tools, tent and cooking kit. Plus, because I'd read about it, duct tape and nylon ties.

The hard-plastic luggage and top-box were brimming and jammed tight.

And last night at exactly midnight with nerves hammering and fear enveloping I had emptied and repacked everything. Twice.

Here and now in the morning, my wife and I discuss my toilet habits. She has years of experience taking children on journeys and toileting them before the off. But I'm wondering, smart in my red wax jacket, about two related things.

Did I realise that I looked like a Mountie, Canadian RCMP? And would a Mountie's wife say in a sweet Canadian drawl, to her man high up on his horse, "Hey Honey, have you been to the toilet for a wee?"

No answer comes. To answer my wife I nod my head, a final kiss and loving hug and I'm ready to mount up too.

Normally the prospect of a long ride and new horizons fills me with excitement; any biker knows that too few hours on the road creates a craving for wind in the face, but this time I am somewhat beset by nerves.

Is it because the bike is still new to me? The Stelvio is a very large machine, I am physically small, and still learning to ride it with confidence.

Or maybe it's because I have spoken to other riders who have ridden through Mongolia and the thought of riding over trackless deserts on my own is just a little daunting.

But here we are, early on this bright and shiny blue skied morning, birdsong at high volume, and I'm ready to leave

Helmet on, gloves on. Gloves off, helmet secured, gloves on. In fitted black jeans with kevlar cladding, my leg is swung over the saddle and then sitting tall with the nerves yammering and fear in the pit of the stomach.

A final contrived smile to hide the stretching of the fear and rolling off the drive onto the road. Nerves quieting, fear leaving, and, with the acceleration, the thrill of adventure beginning.

To Dover, and brief nauticalia. I was a sailor, and indeed a nuclear submariner, in our good Queen's Navy almost fifty years ago. So, I prefer the tradition, and sometimes for cost, to cross the English Channel by ship.

There is an anticipation and a finality about leaving my Island; crossing the sea, disembarking to touch the soil of a new country and knowing, unmistakably, that I'm finally abroad.

For once I'd got the time right for the Ferry with the wait just thirty minutes; motorcycles are no longer at the front of the queue for the off which is a shame but, well, the advantage was only ever minimal.

Boarding. Up the scary clanking metal ramp into this gigantic steel space painted white, blue, and yellow, the occasional patch of rust, and sailors ready to hook up and strap down my motorcycle with me thanking anyone who'd listen that it was dry with no skidding on the deck. It's the mid-morning ferry from Dover to Calais in France.

Sunshine still abounds, blue sky but a bit of a chill and bluster introduced with the ship rocking lightly in the wind.

And usually, at the front on landing, for fear of looking like a laggard or a fool, I ride off at speed. Invariably in the wrong direction.

In fact, the ride to Dortmund was short - about four hundred kilometres - and although I rode through three languages the journey in the countryside was marked only by the general lack of features, other than complying with Continental law by riding on the wrong side of the road.

I wasn't arrested in France for not wearing a Day-Glo jacket.

Nor, dammit, was I arrested and asked for a breath test with the breathalyser and spare light bulbs in a packet. Dammit because I had panic purchased them, just in case, on the Net three days ago.

There was musical interlude, briefly, in Belgium. The motorcycle was flashing its little yellow dashboard light in such an endearing way that I knew more petrol was required. Into a petrol station, with people, which in Belgium is passingly strange. The previous year I'd found Belgian petrol stations that served petrol, air, oil, coffee, hot croissants and umbrellas with nary a human in sight. Full service; but only slots for cards or cash.

So here I am, card outstretched and the dark haired Belgian girl behind the till asking, in a voice not dissimilar to Ms. Bette Midler, if I want to dance in the moonlight. I am taken aback by such a friendly attitude especially as it is daylight outside and the girl is now singing at the top of her voice. I pay, smile and as I leave the store realise Ms. Midler is also singing at the top of her voice, but inside my helmet. And can be heard, for the accompaniment and joining in, on the outside too. A wave from the till and I smile, riding away, as the 'Wind beneath my wings' begins to play over the engine noise.

The cities rolled by too; from the road, the architecture mainly glass and steel with little attempt to uphold and identify with centuries of previous culture.

It may be the wrong side of the road but the wheels are spinning nicely and away from the cities and back in the countryside I'm inhaling bucolic cow, pig, and chicken manure smells that fill the air and are seemingly richer and longer lasting than those in Surrey. No wonder, I thought, we Brits import so much meat and dairy products; viewed up close, Le Continent is just one enormous farm.

The motorways streamed by, the language changes but so far understandable. No crowds to wave at, or to commune with; the weather now dull and grey so I guess the crowds are indoors watching the daytime TV.

So, all's well. Except. And it is quite a big exception. NDrive, my phone mounted Satnav software is more than ever completely crazed. It runs for ten minutes and retires hurt, thence crashing the phone in pique.

I had decided, this journey, to avoid the expense of maps and trust ever more firmly in technology. I hadn't even bothered to print some Google maps. Except one, on one page of A4, delineating, in very small scale, a route from London to Vladivostok.

The advantage being that it fits in the tank bag folder, the distance doesn't look that far and it didn't seem to matter that Vladivostok was not the desired destination. Bing.com seems to be a better mapping tool than Google incidentally – Bing takes you across borders, whilst Google adds hundreds of kilometres by finding a route around.

Being map-less hasn't been a problem previously. I stayed on roads going vaguely in the direction I wanted and put up my tent or found a hotel when I got tired.

Besides, I was looking forward to meeting new friends.

New friends are made at the side of the road when problems dump you there. No problems, no meetings. And, as you've maybe realised, I'm not a dealership tourist.

I'm a couch-surfing tourist. With friends, friends of friends and new friends yet to be met to include those from Couchsurfing, dot com, too.

This Friday, June 1st, I was to stay with Birgit, a talented photographic artist and producer whose work adorns the interweb and several galleries here in her native Germany.

I had arranged to meet Birgit about seven in the evening, calculated as a four-hundred-kilometre ride starting at an hour past noon. But I hadn't put NDrive into the frame and was summarily, and accordingly, punished.

I dialled in the address in Calais; off to the motorway and NDrive collapsed, phone crashed, and, like the sole participant in a TV quiz show I ask myself, "Which motorway?"

I stopped the bike, powered the phone down to reboot, redial in the address.

Through and past Bruges and Ghent and Antwerp and then Essen, heading on for Duisburg

Said process of rebooting NDrive repeats interminably as I rode across flat lands where people spoke in different shades of French perhaps, and almost, to my ear at least, German. Equally annoying the music must be retuned too. I favour tosh for motorways as it's just there to keep me awake; on A roads and the countryside a mix of Opera and original R&B depending on the aspect and the weather. And all this in high speed spurts; with frequent stops to reboot.

And coffee breaks.

I'm always nervous in continental cafes. It's that alien queuing to order and pay in one queue, then off to another to collect the order. I'm not sure what it is that I find so unsettling – the system used, pay and pick up, or trying to buy something when I'm pretending to speak in foreign.

In my home town, you order, get the product and then pay the English-speaking foreigner behind the till.

Finally, to Birgit about nine thirty in the evening, just two and half hours behind the plan.

On ringing the bell a few moments pass and there at the door, resplendent in admiral blue blouse and jeans, Birgit stands.

Middle aged, middle-sized with a waist and still dark blonde she dazzles with bright wide smile and then a huge hug of welcome; a weight lifts and I feel the first moments of real joy since leaving Surrey so many hours, seemingly weeks, ago.

She directs me to rear of the apartment block where I put the bike on the side stand and unload toiletries and change of underwear. I'm here for one night only, no need for a change of outer garments.

She is wonderfully patient, understanding and forgiving now that I've finally arrived at her smart three storied new and brick built apartment block; to make me feel better she confessed immediately that to avoid making mistakes she uses technology as sparingly as possible.

Birgit, wonderful host that she is, had had the grace not to cook or eat until I was there to join to her.

Over dinner: Birgit's interests are wide; her special interests, like mine own, are travelling and photography. I also benefit in the particular as her cooking is based on her travels, and especially her travels in Italy.

She's also travelled a lot in America, and lived there for some time too. We both agreed that a diet of Denny's left a lot to be desired, and the Italian meal before me had the benefits of olive oil, pressed by herself in Tuscany, and garlic; all quick to prepare.

We chatted into the small hours; she had been very ill a couple of years ago and is recovering still. The hospital where she had surgery made a mistake with the blood pumped in her and she has been fighting for compensation ever since.

I thought that the German health system would be close to perfect, but now I discovered it, too, to be as error prone and bureaucracy ridden as every other country.

On the morrow in the morning she insists I take her delicious bread filled with cheese and tomatoes for my lunch. People. Worldwide… just amazing.

ONWARD,
TO THE EAST

When I first decided to travel to Mongolia I thought I would do it in bite sized chunks.

Unless I'm lost I stick to major roads because I seriously dislike riding on fumes deep in the countryside of places where I cannot speak the language, or in darkness, or both, desperately searching for fuel.

I have done too much of it, and the exercise, although perhaps good for the heart, does nothing for my angst, anger management and central nervous system.

In the now, Dortmund to Wroclaw, a gentle amble of a few hundred kilometres, scheduled to arrive at about six in the evening.

Enter NDrive, and an hour and a half wasted riding hither and thither around the city, adjacent countryside and petrol stations trying to find an autobahn; said autobahn apparently only ten kilometres from Birgit's home.

Having finally found the on ramp I rediscovered that in Germany everyone thrashes their cars mercilessly. You can be travelling at speeds that would get you banged up in Britain, but still drivers are flashing their lights and tailgating to get past and onto the next roadblock as soon as they can.

And there was a roadblock; and like a lot of things in this country, it was monumental. All the motorways, it transpired, for fifty kilometres around were snarled up at a complete standstill.

The strange thing was, the ferociously competitive drivers merely sat, without seemingly to complain, accepting the inevitable and waiting for the wreckage to be cleared. Evidently a lorry had caught fire at the conjunction of two motorways so both the main carriageway and the feeder lane came to a halt. The jams spread out like a pebble tossed in a pool and the whole motorway system stopped.

And no-one filtered through the stalled traffic. Except me.

I'm fairly used to traffic filtering. If you live or ride in a city like London it becomes second nature; motorists are aware of bikes coming through and will generally give way. In Germany, this isn't done, so although I could snake between lanes, few cars would move over – it was as if they were paralysed, or perhaps it is illegal.

I was stuck between a car and a truck who were too close and could not, would not move. A voice said over my shoulder "Yer arse is too fat with those panniers, you won't get through."

And so it was that my new friend Kurt introduced himself. Sitting on huge and heavy GS 1200, Kurt was on his second trip round the world. Riding up from South Africa he'd been to his embassy to get some visa fixing done, and here he was riding between the lanes, but without his usually wide panniers.

No more conversation, we're moving and rode between the lanes together. At one point, when NDrive had died yet again, I called to him "Do you know how to get to Gottingen?"

"I'm going there," he grinned, "follow me."

We peeled off at the next junction and Kurt asked if I fancied a country route. "Sure" I said and for next hour we sprinted around twisties in the pine forested foothills of the Weserbergland mountains; great fun and it had the added benefit to me of increasing confidence with handling the bike.

We pulled over for petrol and I listened and learned from his tales of his round the world trips. From South Africa, he rode north up to Murmansk, turned around and went through most of Asia then Europe, winding up in Germany. He acquired a girlfriend and was about to work a short contract offshore to finance the next trip down to Australia.

A really cool guy; brimming with confidence, humour, and South African get up and go.

He took me to the motorway on-ramp and roared off. Ride safe Kurt.

Onward past Leipzig, remembered as a point on a dial on my crystal set to which I listened deep in the night under the bedclothes as an eleven-year-old boy, and then through fire stormed Dresden which, I learned in school, was a justified and just retaliation in a war gone by. I don't think we were always taught the truth.

Onward still, the motorway clear, crossing a border, and now on a normal road, with a smile and a nod to the Handmaidens of Joy waiting for work in the forest in the middle of the day with the rain lubricious around them.

On toward Wroclaw with NDrive in a state of permanent collapse and thick juicy rain permeating the waterproofed wax jacket and a stop too late to protect, already wet, but waterproofs were struggled on; I rode on in the gathering night.

I was staying with Couchsurfing contact Marta, an MA student reading music and an MBA.

I found the turnoff and plunged into the unlit blackness of the potholed countryside, but, after riding through the village thrice said to Marta on the phone "I can't find you." And she said "Wait, I'll switch the lights on." Out of the darkness an elegant country house appeared, a house that would have graced the pages of Horse & Hound had it been for sale in England. Three storeys high it stood, and equally wide, tall columns and an intricate curlicued iron work gate opening to reveal the drive.

Tall, dark and elegant herself, Marta came down the steps and waved, directing me to rear of the house.

Me, short and weary, wearing mud soaked waterproofs, climbed off the bike. "How very nice to meet you." said Marta in perfect English. "Hello." I croaked.

Ten minutes later, sitting in a kitchen big enough for a matched pair of epee fencers performing their stuff, eating an enjoyable meal prepared and delivered by Marta's mother, I learned of how Marta commutes between three universities in different cities to follow her education. She is a gifted pianist and would love to do nothing more, but said it would not pay enough. Decisions had been taken; complete the MBA and probably work doing mergers and acquisitions for a bank or similar corporation. Lucky the bank that employs her.

The family live a few hundred metres away in a smart modern home. The country house had been owned for many generations, but the cost of modernising and draught proofing was so prodigious they built another and moved in.

Marta lives in this beautiful house alone with her horses; in the morning her mother, bright, breezy and forcing more food upon me, asking advice about planting in the garden – one of my nineteen previous careers, that of landscape design – having been mentioned the previous evening. The younger sister, after getting over initial shyness, chatted volubly in English talking about her school, an eighty-kilometre daily commute and her plans… to be happy. In Paris.

Meantime Marta is planning to ride her horse to Mongolia although passing through customs posts could be something of a challenge; but if it can be done, Marta is sure to try.

TECHNICALLY EQUIPPED

Off now, and looking for a new built motorway, this time with notes from Google maps to get me to the border helpfully printed by Marta. The heading remained east to the Ukrainian border another four hundred kilometres away.

But sitting on the bike, somehow arrived on a rutted track watching a farmer happily ploughing his field on his little red tractor, it occurred to me that the God's of Navigation were probably having a day off, or merely giggling at my plight.

I shouted to him "Warsaw?" Not that I wanted to go to Warsaw, but knowing no other town that was pronounceable I thought if I went in that direction I might bisect a main road and head east instead of the southward course I was currently travelling.

The farmer smiled, waved and pointed back the way I had come. I went off-road; well, a gentle semi-circle in his newly ploughed field, waved an apology and set off north.

The small village I had passed in the wrong direction five minutes earlier appeared to be deserted still. Polish villages that sit bestride main roads are smart and clean and have two storey buildings, TV satellite dishes, shops and flashing road signs. Off the beaten track the houses are small, one storey, and uniformly grey, linked umbilically with overhead power cables, and, for the relatively rich, phone lines too.

But, there was a minimarket here, it's door opened and security grilles pinned back against the concrete panelled wall.

I sought inside more defined directions as NDrive had failed completely, and this village didn't show on the carefully printed map.

To the counter and the man who stood guard over endless shining rows of bottled vodka, beer, and a few vegetables to ask, with my helmet removed and in my best English accent, "Warsaw, pazhalsta?" as I knew, at his age, he'd probably learnt Russian in school.

He looked at me, looked away, and looked at me again. "Warsaw?" I repeated. He repeated his looking at, and away, but faster. I knew this now to be a negative shaking of the head.

To myself I thought "Godammit, doesn't he even know in which direction his capital city is?"

And thought again that if I was standing in a corner shop deep in the English countryside, and a grubby foreigner arrived wearing an equally grubby tar stained red wax jacket on a mud plastered motorcycle asking questions in a language not my own what would I do? Why, I'd take him outside and point. Point to anywhere, just to get rid of him.

Which is just what the shopkeeper did, and in ignorance, but with a more hopeful heart, I rode in the direction given.

Months later, on the way back from Mongolia I discovered that Warsaw is pronounced Vashava, but right now I'm back on a bisected road with some good grey concrete and the wheels are spinning east.

I caught up for lost time with some spirited riding until, on the outskirts of the city of Zabrze, and just as I was overtaking some fellow Brit bikers riding in a pack of four, I felt the back wheel start to weave.

I slowed down, the weave got worse. Fearing what might happen I pulled over onto the hard shoulder and looked down at the deflated rear tyre. The Brits roared past with nary a glance; serves me right for overtaking at speed.

Two of the characters in my head were crying fat tears. Another, more optimistic, chuckled and said "Ahh... an opportunity to turn a crisis into something worse." I had, after all, brought a tyre repair kit with me.

First thing, get the bike up on the centre stand. But with all the weight in the plastic luggage there was no chance. Besides, this was not a real hard shoulder on the two-lane motorway. A hundred metres ahead was an on ramp. I got back on the bike and managed to get it up the ramp, heading the wrong way.

I stood looking at the rear tyre thinking "Now what?" when a small car pulled up, going down the ramp. My next new best friend got out and said "Hi, I'm a biker, can I help?"

My height, but muscled, dark haired with a smile like a beacon, it turned out that Jack wasn't just a biker, he was a local icon, renowned for near vertical wheelies and stoppies.

We looked over the tyre together but couldn't see anything immediately. "I'll make a call." he said.

Now this was Saturday afternoon and all good bike shops were closed with the real players off to a rally nearby.

Waiting for a call back, and on mutual agreement, we decided I should ride the bike fifteen-hundred metres to Jack's home where we could pull the wheel and take a proper look.

A precarious short ride and we pulled into his drive and parked the bike. "Look," he said, "this is my first day off for a month and I promised my fiancée that I would take her shopping for an hour. You'll stay here tonight and we'll try to fix it later or in the morning."

By now I was sitting in an enormous open plan sitting room, served mugs of tea and surrounded by dishes of Polish chocolate. I wasn't going anywhere.

Jack and Monica kindly curtailed their shopping trip and were back in an hour. We headed to the garage, him to do, me to watch. A member of the local biking fraternity called on the phone; he had a Metzler of the right size in stock, would I like it?

You bet!

Spannering and banging and the wheel was pulled and we're off to the shop for a tyre.

To discover two previous puncture repairs, one of which was leaking. On discovery of which expletives expressed and repeated and new rubber going on fast at virtually cost price. Handshakes, smiles and biker farewells and we're off back to Jack's.

Wheel on, Jack still insistent I stay the night, and the next act of generosity began. It transpires that Jack is a partner in a hotel and insists we go to try some superior Silesian food.

The hotel, Zielony Ogrod, – Green Garden – was simply stunning. Set in landscaped gardens with fountains and water features it had been opened just five months. Entrance lobby, high ceilinged, light and spacious, pale grey marble staircase, classic-meets-modern designed and built.

The hotel was owned and run by Jack, his sister, two of his cousins, and his uncle.

Jack ran the hotel; his cousin Richard ran the restaurant with his sister managing the back office.

I asked to look around and was taken on a tour of three dining rooms, an assortment of bedrooms with uber-cool design touches everywhere and staff equally well-mannered and attentive and saying "Hello."

Inspection over, we entered the garden and found a table in the sun. Jack walked me through the English menu and I ordered, on recommendation, Silesian beef.

I do not claim a sophisticated palate; more, now, is the order of the day. But here was melt in the mouth beef served with the lightest ever dumplings and a side of diced red cabbage. Simple and perfectly cooked. More, now, was offered; but would mean buttons undone and belt notches to be loosened. I was still on best behaviour so I refrained. It was enough and more to be sitting in this ultra-smart hotel, eating enjoyable food and talking to an enlightened, enthusiastic and highly motivated biker – karma of the road is strong.

I had to sing for my supper though. The food is all grown and purchased locally; the chef makes his own sausages and smokes the meats outdoors in a specially built smoke house. Singing for my supper was actually a taste test of the smoked hams, beef, pork and sausages.

The sausage and smoked sirloin won. And as we left the hotel a package of my preferences mysteriously appeared "For the journey." Jack smiled.

We went for a brief tour of the city. This is Silesia, land of hunting and coal so I was pleasantly surprised how green the city was and how the coal mines seemed to be in the centre of everything. As an industrial city, it has not lost its roots; it's being spruced up and reborn extremely well.

The next morning, Sunday, bright and early I got back on the road, retracing my route and smiling as I went down the self-same on-ramp on which I was stranded earlier.

About five hundred metres later the rear wheel was weaving at a terrifying rate. I stopped, got off and checked the back wheel. Flat, no pressure, nothing. Another five hundred metres further a service station beckoned, I rode with a flat tyre and parked next to the air pump.

After five fruitless minutes the attendant came and kindly changed the valve on the air compressor. Nothing Nada. No pressure.

Not a man to panic under stress I called Jack and handed the stress to him. Couple of hours later he arrived - having arranged for someone to take over his work shift - and made the same inspection that I had done; except he saw the problem immediately. A spoke had retracted into the wheel; with a tubeless tyre it spelt immediate disaster as the air just flowed out.

Phone calls made, messages dropped into the local biker's forum. Meantime, off came the wheel, into his car and by the time we had done this a message came back from a biker who owned a tyre shop that he would try to fix it that afternoon. And this on a Sunday!

The owner gave up his day of rest to come to work to help a biker in trouble. He'd brought his daughter in her push chair to overview the situation and as he opened the workshop doors he pointed to his wife's motorcycle sitting proudly on the floor.

After some tries it was obvious the spoke couldn't be salvaged so his plan B was to fill the hole on the rim with silicone and a metal patch bolted on. Tyre filled with air, pressure tested, perfect.

I was not allowed to pay anything; this perfect stranger said, like others on the road, "Send me some pictures of Mongolia" and shooed us away.

Back to the motorway petrol station we had the wheel back on fast and I told Jack to go, and that everything was fine, but he insisted on staying until the bike was fired and running.

I switched it on, dashboard lit up with all its fairy lights - plus another which was new to me.

The Electronic Command Unit controls all the bike's engine electrics. No ECU, no firing up, no lights, no go anywhere.

Jack got back on the phone to one of his buddies who got on the net and Googled "Moto Guzzi Stelvio ECU failure." He came back with the news that a local Stelvio owner had a similar problem; it was a mini fifteen-amp fuse in the cockpit.

Sighing with exasperation we checked the bike over. The culprit, in fact, was the rear break sensor cable. When we put the brake unit back on to the rear wheel we had inadvertently crushed the cable and shorted the system.

Jack stripped it all back and wrapped black tape around the separate wires.

Then we checked all the fuses, no easy job because they were located under the dashboard. Dashboard was removed, fuses checked. One fifteen-amp fuse had died; I hadn't been able to get any fifteen amp replacements in the UK before I left so we stuck a ten amp in and hoped for the best.

Tried the starter, cool, everything firing except there were no lights. Off came the dashboard, fuse check on the HID lights – aha, the fuse had melted when we shorted the system. Replaced fuse, put dashboard back on, fired up – lights on!

This time I insisted that Jack should go and finally he did.

I got all the bags and panniers onto the bike, tied everything down... and couldn't find the keys.

I had left the keys in the tool storage compartment under the saddle. Couldn't open the saddle because it had to be opened with the key that was locked under the saddle.

Fortunate indeed that I finally remembered the spare key. Off came the bags, saddle unlocked, keys recovered, bags secured in place. Fired up the bike, no lights!

Over the next hour, I removed and replaced all the fuses a couple of times. The motorway police turned up, speaking perfect English and offered to make a replacement fuse with a paperclip. For which I thanked them, but at that very moment Jack called; he'd sent me a text which I hadn't answered so he phoned to make sure I was ok.

I told him about the lights and he said there was nothing for it but to bring the bike back to his house and we could check in his garage where he had tools and equipment.

I rode back with a heavy heart. Jack was incredibly kind but this was really going the extra mile for the Brotherhood.

Back in his garage dozens of solutions were tried. One problem is that the headlights don't come on until the engine is running. So, for everything we tried we had to take off the dash board to access lights and fuses, do a fix, put the dashboard back on and so on.

Jack's neighbour came by and piled in to help too. Finally, around nine o clock I said, that's it, I'll take it to a specialist in the morning.

I fired the bike up one more time – bingo, full power HID headlights.

Wow! I tried it twice more and each time the lights came up with no problems.

Handshakes, smiles, real pleasure at solving an intractable problem.

Gratefully we all went off to bed ready for an early start.

Zabrze To Kyiv, Almost.

The motorway was good for another two hundred kilometres and then became the E40, Europe's longest continuous road.

Now it's mainly only two lanes passing through small towns and villages. There was no point in riding fast; it was raining so hard that visibility was less than a hundred metres and the headlights had failed again; I was using the fog lamps at full beam and just rode with a prayer in my head until I reached the border.

Both countries, Poland and Ukraine, are jointly hosting the Euro 2012 and expect a lot of cross border road traffic. Certainly, both crossing points were courteous, smart and quick. A lot of training, particularly on the Ukrainian side, had obviously been put in place. Ukrainian border police and customs actually smiled and said welcome; a far cry from the bribery machine still in place the previous year when I stood here for a full ten minutes as the Border Control riffled through my passport, checked each page under a special light then riffled some more. In the end, I stepped up and said. "Now look here my man, if it's good enough for the Queen of England, it should be good enough for you." And strangely enough, with no money proffered, he gave me passport and with a scowl, jerked his head as a signal to go.

In the now, and with NDrive still less than perfect, I was following road signs. I can read a little Russian and Ukrainian so it was not too hard; except I managed to get lost on the outskirts of Lviv.

Lviv is a lovely medieval city which I promised myself I would never return to when riding a bike. Two years back I had visited on my Victory Vegas cruiser and found the cobbled streets and tramlines, charming to a pedestrian, to be a nightmare on a bike. And in the wet, on a top heavy Stelvio, not the place I wanted to be.

Whilst I was stopped at the side of the road frantically cursing and stabbing at my Sat Nav one of the local Brotherhood pulled over on a cool yellow Honda cruiser. I got off my bike, walked over and he introduced himself as Alexei. Alexei had some great technology on his tank bag – a printed map on which he showed me the ring road around the city and the correct turn off.

Gratefully I shook his hand, he roared off, and I retraced my route. So quite how I found myself in the centre of the city, in the wet, on the cobbles, I really don't know.

I was in full gear under waterproofs, hot, sweating, frustrated and tired. I didn't see the oncoming bus until the last moment. I swerved and braked and saw sky, dirt, sky, dirt, sky and had difficulty breathing. The bike lay in the road leaking petrol, I lay in the road leaking air from my lungs thinking "What next?" when out of the crowd a woman said in clear English, "It's ok, we are bikers, we have called some friends." Within moments I was surrounded with help. I managed to stand up, the bike uprighted and pushed off the road onto the pavement.

An ambulance arrived and I was hustled inside for a check. I had excruciating pain in my ribs but the adrenalin was still running high and dealt with the thresholds of pain. One thing I didn't want to do, having seen at first hand the inside of Ukrainian State hospitals before, was to end up in one now. Immediately the paramedic's prodding had finished I signed a release note and got out of the vehicle.

What I needed was a cigarette and some mechanical help.

As I stood shaking and disoriented the Brotherhood was already in action.

Together we inspected the motorcycle and saw the front wheel had a buckled rim, two spokes had come adrift, one of the fog lamps was bent, some scratches on the panniers and the top box was ripped from its mounting.

The bus driver meantime had called the police, mandatory for any accident of any size in Ukraine. The bikers said, "Don't sign anything until we have looked at it."

A few minutes later an additional team, Loshki and his girlfriend Yara, arrived on an Africa Twin followed by Alexei – the same guy who gave me directions earlier.

Alexei shook his head woefully – "I told you…" he said with a wry smile.

Loshki took charge of things quickly. Statements were made and translated; the bus driver made vigorous swerving movements, the Police pointed to a give way road sign.

In Ukraine, bureaucracy rules everything. For any road traffic accident where people are hurt there has to be a court hearing soon after. Soon after this I wanted to be nine thousand kilometres away so Loshki went into bat.

Money changed hands, new statements appeared, no problems, I could go.

With perfect timing, more of Loshki's friends arrived in a Ukrainian styled vintage Dormobile van kitted out for bike recovery; six bikers pushed the bike into the van, tied it down and off we went.

The workshop was small but brand new; the guys had only been in business since January; they were all bikers and eager to help. A more detailed look at the damage was carried out. The front wheel rim was bent; two spokes had become unmoored because the aluminium housing was broken. Fortunately, I had picked up the broken piece of housing when I was trying to prove to the police exactly where I had come off - I'd handed it over to Motorush mechanics earlier.

They discovered the problem with the lights – the fuse housing had melted and died too – but sorting out the wheel and the two broken spokes in the front wheel is not so simple. Then it also became apparent that the tyre wall had damage too; I'd bought this new a few hundred kilometres ago in Poland but now it was unusable.

I asked the guys to check the brakes and change the oil. "No problem, will be ready soon."

All good, lift and shift, and I'm taken to Loshki and Yara's apartment, told to sit down, worry about nothing, all will be fine.

With some tea inside me and painkillers taken I started to relax.

Thirty minutes later the doorbell rang and the first of a dozen bikers arrived to see the 'crazy English' and have a party.

This was real fun, road stories exchanged, pictures and videos reviewed, advice flowing back and forth. Such open outgoing people – amazingly generous and kind. Strangely enough most of these dyed-in-the-wool bikers were in IT and wives and girlfriends did things in the Arts.

Four days later I'm still in Loshki and Yara's apartment. They have really put themselves out for me in many, many ways. This is a well-kept but small apartment so I'm on a couch… yes, it turns out they're Couch-surfers too!

For me, my two cracked ribs were getting better all the time, I could almost breathe as well as cough. I kept drinking delicious black chai and continued the anxious wait for the workshop to call.

The guys at Motorush did a fine job.

The bent wheel from the accident three days earlier was straightened but there was a small air leak from a used tubeless tyre they'd put on as a replacement. The best solution was to put in an inner tube; which they did.

They'd also sorted the broken fog lamp and main lights – the fuse and its holder melted away, some fibreglass repairs in the cockpit, changed the brake pads and oil, the new used front tyre. One of the Lviv Brotherhood had donated a Givi rear fixing for the broken top box; and thank the gods for the donation, otherwise it would be Mongolia with gaffer tape.

Not content with fixing all this and charging less per day than the dealer at home charges per hour, they invited me to stay with them for the evening and come to their barbecue. Another twelve hours for my ribs to continue healing was not be sneezed at so the acceptance was grateful, and fast.

The barbecue was delicious; properly cooked food with a vast range of sliced and spiced vegetables.

The wives were there with their husbands and I talked to Anton's wife. A very clever and sophisticated woman, she had spent seven years training at University to become a Doctor. After five years in practice, she is a specialist but I cannot remember what in, she now earns less than a third of the minimum wage in the UK.

When I asked her why she did not move to the West to earn more money she said that Ukraine is her country; she became a Doctor to help the sick, not seek large amounts of money.

People still blow me away at every turn.

Next morning, Saturday, came the dawn with a dull grey finish just like foggy Albion. I put my kit together, strapped on the bags and boxes, now held together with shiny grey duct tape, and made ready to leave. Out of nowhere appeared Loshki and Yara. They and Sasha, owner of Motorush, said they were all going to see me safely to the motorway.

The bike was running well although I was having to relearn confidence after the spill. Loshki and Yara peeled off after five kilometres – they were going to Bulgaria and points west on a journey of their own.

Sasha and I continued onward until he pulled into a petrol station. There, waiting to meet us was Vitalii. He and his girlfriend Tatiana were the two people who first pulled me off the road after the accident and called in the Lviv Brotherhood.

Tatiana gave me a keepsake, a teddy bear, and once more I was humbled by thoughtfulness and generosity of these people; from complete strangers to good friends in a matter of moments.

With that, I said goodbye and followed Sasha another twenty kilometres to the main highway to Kyiv.

We said goodbye in a cafe adorned with Soviet cars and motorcycles, a fitting end to this stage of my journey.

The Lviv Brotherhood is not a formal club; it's a bunch of guys and women who are open hearted and generous and who come together to party, ride and when the occasion arises, step in to help in a crisis.

Truly genuine people, I won't forget them for a long time to come. And I was learning more Karma of the road at first hand.

And Then It Rained

The grey morning hadn't brightened at all.

In fact, the skies ahead had blackened, rumbles of thunder and the odd flash of lightening were on the horizon ahead of me. But I was in too much pain to get off the bike and put on wet weather gear, so I just kept going.

The road switched its designation between the M06 and the E40. The M06 is sometimes a dual carriageway and sometimes an eight-lane blacktop.

As it rushed through the countryside, cattle, horses and people cross wherever they see fit. The speed limit is one hundred and ten k.p.h, but you wouldn't know that from the insane speeds of tiny Ladas and huge SUV's whipping past.

Villages and towns are strung out along the roadside. In villages, the houses are usually one storey, painted white and decorated yellow and blue in the colours of the national flag. Electricity arrives from overhead cables, storks nest on the power and telephone poles. Smoke curls from chimneys, even though it's June.

Small churches, usually painted white are surmounted by ubiquitous shining azure blue or gold onion shaped domes. More are being built as the economy improves and the Orthodox Church extends it influence everywhere.

I had no special time schedule to get to Kyiv, a ride of five hundred and fifty kilometres. I took in the views and looked out for cops.

Unbeknownst to most, Ukraine is, after Russia, the second largest country in Europe.

Mountainous in the southwest, hills in the north and the remaining grass steppe, now cultivated, is bisected by mighty rivers flowing north to south. The horizons seem endless.

The modern trunk roads running east to west were mainly constructed for the Soviet Army to transit troops to the west in the wars.

Bimbling along at no great speed I used the technique that Ukrainians call "Follow the beacon." In a nutshell, you stay with traffic at legal speeds until someone in a hurry gets frustrated and bullies you out of the way. You fall in behind and follow at a safe distance so that he or she can take the rap when the law steps in. Works pretty well; two of my 'beacons' were stopped to chat to the police.

The bad thing was the storm ahead. As I rode into it, the rain became torrential. Visibility dropped to a hundred metres or less and I simply didn't feel like pushing it harder. Every fifty kilometres, or when the rain got worse, I stopped and had some coffee.

In one small village in the middle of nowhere they showed me to a table, put out a table cloth, had me sit down – dripping from head to foot – whilst a pretty blonde waitress served me a delicious doppio. With sun shining and birds singing I could have been in Italy, not chasing a storm into Kyiv.

Another three hundred kilometres riding the trailing edge of the storm. Finally, I rode through it and then it caught me up but by now I had entered flag bedecked Euro 2012 crazed Kyiv. I rode straight past the Euro Camp, well on its way to being recognised internationally as one of the most disorganised campsite venues ever, and not just because of the cold water and mud; the Swedes even brought their own Police Force with them.

In the rain, I missed the slip road. As I rode deeper into the city on the main road from Lviv to Kyiv the slip road should have eased me off to the left for the kilometre to the apartment in which I stay. If you want to know where, it's near the Harley Davidson dealership.

I was fiddling with the Sat Nav, and rode straight past; then spent thirty minutes looking for a route back.

It's the strawberry season and in amongst the crowds of footie fans I could see, sitting on stools on the side of the street, the Babushkas selling strawberries, potatoes, vodka, fake brand cigarettes.

I always think of Kyiv as a mini Paris. The centre, around Khreshchatyk and Maidan Square, the latter being internationally famous as the centre of the Orange revolution, has a huge underground shopping mall built so that shoppers can continue to buy in sub-zero temperatures. Above ground is a massive glass edifice that in my mind I liken to the Pompidou centre in Paris. Statues, neon ads and fountains abound, and, being the commercial heart of the city, McDonald's has two outlets almost within spitting distance. Strangely, the Ukrainian fast food shops seem to sell mainly vegetarian meals with fries.

Khreshchatyk, the main street where the western Brands sell their overpriced wares, was flattened in the Second World War and then rebuilt by German POWs. It has a faintly Empire/Hanseatic 1950's look about it, surrounded by Stalin built art deco blocks.

Khreshchatyk is a great place to people watch. At the weekends people from the surrounding villages flood in to gaze at the shops and gawp, like me, at the native Kyivans.

Ukrainians are mainly tall and slim and have two fairly distinct ethnic variations. From the western half of the country they are dark haired, dark eyed and have long straight noses like the characters depicted in the religious icons. It seems they are descendants of the Scythians, the original settlers who arrived here in 3000 B.C.

From the east of Ukraine, the people are equally tall but blonde and have the wide cheekbones and turned up noses.

This group are more likely descendants of the Vikings who established Kyiv, and Kyivan-Rus in 882 AD.

Both ethnicities live peaceably, except in the east, but off-times separated by language, of which there are two. In Kyiv and the east it is Russian, whilst in the west, Ukrainian is the tongue preferred. Ukrainian has been the official language, and taught in all schools since the Orange Revolution, but only the young are capable of speaking both languages. And are pleased to verbally confuse mono-linguistic parents.

THE BIKERS
OF KYIV

I'd delivered the gift of smoked beef to my office.

This pleasant duty done, and now that I was organised in Kyiv, I thought I should get the steering looked at.

It hadn't felt right since my off in Lviv, more vibration through the bars than I was used to. Of course, you can't just go off to a bike shop, you need to check out the bikerhood first.

One of the guys in the office knew a biker, which in turn led me to two brilliant guys, Ivan and Vladimir. Vladimir is a full member, and Ivan a prospect, of The Silver Bullets; the oldest established biker club in Kyiv.

I got the bike to their workshop; if you need it, it's a couple of blocks behind Kyiv's central railway station. You can reach them on the phone – they'll talk you in as they both speak excellent English.

I explained the symptoms as I was worried about the geometry, but after a thorough check they decided it was just a question of balancing the front wheel – I hadn't had this done when the front tyre was replaced in Lviv.

The wheel was removed in a matter of moments and Vlad took it to a tyre master a few blocks away returning in thirty with the wheel and the tyre balanced and true.

Next, a look at the vibration of levers for brake and clutch. To remove the play, he fettled some washers from a beer bottle of plastic and slid the retaining pin through them. Fine result, the play was removed, and the vibration gone. For a while.

Refusing any payment for their time; they flatteringly said it was payment enough to meet a foolhardy lone English biker riding to Mongolia.

Great guys, and not to be forgotten. And they weren't, days later, when I called them for help.

To a biker's bar named Route 66 to see what I can find out about the road to Siberia – and especially from Ashot, the man who rode two back-to-back Iron Butt rides on the Trans-Siberian Highway from Kyiv to Vladivostok. And back. Just eleven thousand kilometres each way.

Ashot also organises, every June, http://tarasovagora.ua/ the best biker Rally in Ukraine. I'd visited riding my Victory Vegas the previous year.

About the road, "It is easy." he says. "The entire road is now tarmacadam, but the trucks are destroying the surface; so best go now before it is wrecked once more."

So I did, the very next day.

OF GANGSTERS

Getting out of cities when you don't understand the traffic signs is never easy; particularly when your start point is in the suburbs. Moreover, NDrive, the world's most fallible Sat Nav software was still sulking so it was going to be my personal navigation skills or an escort out of town.

Natalie, my business partner in Kyiv was fabulous; she gave up her morning and drove ahead out to the E38, pointed me East and waved me onward.

Natalie is the second strong woman who re-ordered my life. The first, my wife, put up with my drinking and bizarre behaviour for ten years of marriage, and five without, before she joined Al-Anon and gently, firmly and with deep love altered my course and set me on the road to sober recovery.

Being sober is such an amazing gift; the very least it does is to grant you the tools to deal with life in technicolour, as opposed to blackout.

In 2002 or thereabouts I started a loose relationship, that of client and supplier, with some web developers in Kharkov, hard by the Russian border in deepest east Ukraine.

They were very, very clever and reasonably priced. When I flew there to meet them I discovered they worked from tobacco stained crumbling apartments; their computers tied up with string.

And thought, if they are prepared to work so hard in these conditions then I am prepared to work with them.

They spoke good English; had to, how else could they be taught in University the reverse engineering of Microsoft's finest software?

I worked with them for a couple of years through some admittedly tough times. Software engineers would complete a project and then leave the country with their new-found skills to worship Mammon in the west. When they left, there was no history on the project; even minor changes required new training.

The Ukrainian project manager, a truly talented and able young man, decided to move to the capital, Kyiv, and try his luck anew.

Once there he suggested we open a company together, to include the developers in Kharkov, but hire permanent people as well. We opened, and for a while, we prospered.

But these were dangerous times in Kyiv. Corruption was everywhere engrained at the top and bottom of everyday life. There was no rule of law; judges took money with the same alacrity as cops and other officials of state.

Into this vacuum stepped the gangsters.

A story is told, first hand. A friend's father, a successful TV producer; a man of good reputation and relative wealth, backed by an American broadcaster, he had his own show delivering home grown content to the local market.

Until one day, arriving at his office, he met two men already inside. Both men were shaved bald, wore black suits, black t-shirts and heavy gold bangles. No brand name showed on the shirts

Being the owner he asked why they were there inside his office without permit or invitation. He was told they liked the show and the money thus generated and had decided to own it themselves. So they did. The investors knew nothing, nor the owners of the station, but the show had new owners. The Producer kept his life and the debts for him to repay.

This is the country, remember, where a Minister of State committed suicide officially, by shooting himself in the back of the head, twice.

Meantime, in my small world, in 2004, my ambitious and then business partner, having read of the gangsters in government and out, was doing the self-same thing. To me.

I arrived from London by air, went to the office and found it empty. No desks, chairs, computers or people. Nothing.

What to do in a country full of gangsters, corruption and a language I did not understand?

The Embassy? They talked of Wimbledon, strawberries and of tea. Out of our jurisdiction, sorry old chap we're diplomatic, not in the business of recovering small businesses stolen.

Fortunately, I had the cell phone number of one of the kidnapped developers.

I'd met Natalie on-line in a previous year as a translator / interpreter with a computer and mathematics degree. I phoned, gave her the number and asked if she could locate my man and an explanation as to actions already and illegally undertaken.

She made the call, told me of the kidnap, the stealing of equipment and that the business had a new sole owner; my previously partnered project manager.

I hadn't got involved in the local expatriate community so my sole English speaking network, Embassy apart, was my twelve-step programme. But what you are about to learn is not normally the business of twelve step programmes.

I went to a meeting and approached an Australian who had shared his past from which I knew he was the man for the job.

Early in the morning my Australian friend, two large members of his staff and myself in the vanguard, travelled in a van to the address of the business sequestered.

Some shouting and shoving at the door and we were inside, equipment collected and into the van and a message to the developers to standby for news.

Lift and shift to an office in the city centre that I'd rented the night before;

equipment installed and developers contacted and re-contracted to work in the new location.

To Natalie on the phone to offer a job; would she run the new business for me? Brave person, she did and made it all legal with tax to the correct authorities and rent and people paid with clients managed, internationally, with no knowledge of the temporary breakdown in service.

Eight years on and it gets better as Natalie had professed a liking for bikes and enjoyed speed and travel from the pillion seat.

In three years' time, she will pass her motorcycle test. But that is a book in the future.

Karma
Of The Road

Natalie gone and about thirty minutes out of Kyiv I'm in a layby fiddling and prodding the Sat Nav when a BMW GS650 pulled up by behind me. After all the help I had received the least I could do was to amble over and offer assistance if it was needed.

It wasn't. Eugenia, for that was her name, didn't need any help; she had a map and was looking at her directions by road. A map. Being read by a good looking English speaking Russian girl. And yes, she was going to the Russian border.

Evidently, she was one of thousands of Russian bikers who had been to a bike rally in Crimea and were all now riding home. It's a fifteen hundred kilometre journey each way from Moscow to the Crimea; you need to be serious if you're going to this rally.

She was heading for Moscow and when she offered to lead me to the border I didn't take long to agree.

Eugenia led off at a good pace and we swept into a long right hand curve going due east. Perfect, until two hundred metres later the GS650 chain expired, fortunately falling on the road and not wrapping itself around the rider.

I stopped, collected the chain and walked up the hard shoulder to where she sat with a distraught look on her face.

"What do you when this happens?" she asked.

She was stranded in a foreign country with a broken chain, no local contacts, talking to an equally stranded non-mechanical Englishman.

"No problem," I said, "we call the Brotherhood." Which we did, and the two wheeled Saint Ivan said he'd be there in an hour.

Meantime, a Russian rider on a Suzuki Intruder peeled off the road and pulled up. From his face and stature he was clearly from far eastern Russia, although it transpired that, after rallying for days, he was Moscow bound too.

Dima, his name, took a look at the chain, got out a hammer and set about trying to remove a link. "Aaah." I thought, "Obvious, really" whilst mentally blessing Moto Guzzi's trouble free shaft drive. The link refused to be removed with the tools he had and at that very moment Ivan called Eugenia to confirm the breakdown point and that he would be about forty-five minutes. He was coming in his car with proper tools and kit.

It was now about four in the afternoon and I still had to go through customs at the border and make the four hundred and fifty kilometres to Voronezh, Russia. Do-able, I thought, in five hours. However, I couldn't just leave Eugenia on the side of the road with scary looking biker so I said I would stay.

I forgot, of course, that Dima was her countryman, could obviously mend bikes and was a lot more useful than me.

She insisted that I go. Meantime Dima looked at his map and helpfully said I should turn back southwest and cross the border east at Sumy as it was a more direct route to Voronezh. I knew better of course; hadn't I spent hours on Google Maps selecting the best routes?

With more Russian riders powering down the road I knew I could tag along and follow them to the border.

Ivan was on his way, Eugenia again insisted I went; I was as useful as a snowball in hell, so I did just that.

Falling in behind three Honda office blocks blazing with light and wearing Russian plates, I tore off with them towards the Russian border. These guys knew no fear – their riding style was fast, precise and the hell with the crooked Ukrainian traffic cops. Mostly touching three figures of speed I followed them happily as they cleared traffic before them like an armada of outriders carving tracks over the horizon.

Until I realised they were heading for a different border.

Eighty kilometres of fantastic and spirited riding, but all in the wrong direction. My eight-o-clock arrival in Voronezh was looking less likely.

I turned around, and at a less speedy pace retraced my route until I found signs for the border.

Riding The Russian Night

Huge lines of massive trucks marked the route to the border post; I rode past until I saw the Ukrainian soldier handing out transit tickets. I got mine and rode slowly to the Ukrainian passport police. Just before I reached them I saw what I was looking for – Green Card insurance on sale.

You can't buy a pan Eastern European Green Card unless you are registered as resident. This means, as a Brit, you have to buy it at every border, and the price is always a stinger.

What's worse though, is the corrupt border officials who require a bribe before they let you through without it. So, this time, I'd be prepared. I stopped the bike, went to the closest insurance seller and asked for insurance for Russia. No problem except I had little cash and cards were not accepted. The sales guy pointed to the Border post buildings "Bank ATM." he said.

I walked to the border police; a very pretty and feminine female soldier kind of understood my mission and let me through. Inside the border post was a bank; no ATM, all they did was exchange money.

I asked an important looking man for help – he passed me on to three women customs officers who all struggled to help in English. But couldn't

Mission aborted I went back to get the bike. The salesman pointed to the next insurance sales cabin… ho hum, why not try.

I went into the cabin and explained that I wanted insurance.

"Ok." said the saleswoman in English. She started to fill out the form and I asked "Skolka?" meaning "How much?"

The reply was eighteen euros; my problem was I only had twelve and her office didn't accept credit, debit or any other kind of card either. We chatted for a few minutes; she had good English with an excellent accent but her seldom use of the language had limited her vocabulary. Anyway, I told her the truth; her English was very good.

She asked if I would tell her teacher that she had been speaking to me. Plink plink on the mobile and I was speaking to her English teacher; I complimented her on the teaching she had given her pupil. We spoke for a few moments – she was cooking for a family dinner – and I handed the phone back.

The lovely Natalie, for now I knew her name, gave me a beaming smile and said, "I will make you special insurance for fifteen days for twelve Euros."

Such kindness for a traveller in trouble.

I thanked her, took the certificate and got back on the bike.

Ukrainian police and customs were processed very quickly - mainly because one of the young women I had been speaking to when trying to find an ATM spotted me and personally took my documentation through each section.

The Russian side got very complicated, very quickly.

There are two forms to be filled in. One for the police, one for customs. The police form is in English and Russian. It asks for details on when you are entering and leaving the country and with whom or where you are staying. I didn't have the name of my sponsor so I just made it up. I handed over the form – they didn't bother to check the insurance, entered my bike details from my log book into their computer system, smiled and sent me onward.

Customs was something else again.

Their form is two pages, all in Russian and must be done in duplicate. When I asked the customs officer for some help he pointed to me to a table on which a plastic covered form was Sellotaped down. This form had been completed as a guide, but as the questions in Russian had been completed with answers in Russian it was about as useful for me as if it had been written with a chocolate bar.

I should have known that there would be problems. The officer dealing me was the only guy in the office wearing a hat. Russian forces, be they Army, Navy, Airforce, Border or Customs have an added ten centimetres rise above the peak. To make then look larger and more important I guess. Add self-importance to ten centimetres and you knew there could be problems.

I did my best with the form, with lots of gaps. I took it back to the customs guy who looked at it and then asked the guy next to me in the queue to help me.

My pressed helper was from Bulgaria and couldn't speak Russian or English, but tried. He filled in some of the answers; which answers I copied to the duplicate form with some crossings out and overwriting. Signed, and handed them over.

The passport guy threw a fit. "Perfect!" he said, and tore the forms in half and threw them in a bin before handing me two new forms.

I knew I had to keep cool so I asked for the torn-up forms to be returned so I could copy them again. He understood and with bad grace handed them over.

I duly copied them all out, handed them back and he looked through the form. He pointed out the engine capacity box in which I had written 1100cc. "Nyet" he shouted. "KVA". I crossed out 1100 and put 1.1. "Nyet" he shouted- "perfect, perfect" He crumpled the forms and gave me two more.

I was starting to lose it; but thought, he hadn't invited to me Russia, it was me who wanted to get in.

Lesson to be learned eventually was that the information on the form could be complete nonsense as long as whatever was written was perfect and neat.

After two hours of tomfoolery I gave him one form that was new and one that he had rejected earlier, but there were no deletions or amendments to be seen. He looked them over, stamped my passport and motioned me onward.

What with getting lost, helping the lady biker and form filling I was now six hours late in meeting my host in Voronezh – still four hundred and fifty kilometres east. The time zone had also shifted an hour but I didn't know this until later.

Onward in gathering darkness; the road bad to mediocre. Cafes were shut but petrol stations worked twenty-four hours so I stopped to refill whenever the milometer showed the equivalent of one hundred and fifty kilometres.

This bike's range is between one hundred and ninety and two hundred and twenty-five kilometres but the engine is optimised for fuel at a speed of one hundred and twenty kilometres per hour; there's no chance of riding at that speed on most Russian roads, let alone at night. Sometimes it took three hours to do hundred kilometres.

As a rule of thumb the gap between petrol stations is about seventy kilometres but I became paranoid on a couple of stretches where the petrol stations were a long way apart.

Summer nights in Russia are short but intense. The sun sets about ten thirty and by eleven the huge sky filled with endless stars to wheel around your head.

By two a.m. I was feeling dispirited; cold, hungry and tired from concentrating on the road. I pulled over to a concrete built bus stop with room enough for six which fortunately had both a roof and seat. Laying there alone in the middle of a forest I asked myself what the hell I was doing trying to ride Russian roads at night when everyone had warned me they were dangerous. The danger isn't from robbers or bandits, it's the road quality and Russian driving skills.

A bar of luncheon chocolate found and eaten, the sugar giving me an immediate lift. As I looked at the beauty of the black night and the diamond splintered stars above I dug into my mental reserves and told myself I could do it. I put on some more clothes and my wet weather gear to act as a wind-stopper and got back on the bike.

An hour or so later, around three-thirty, sipping coffee at a petrol station watching a bunch of teenagers partying around their cars with the edge of dawn breaking. Another fifteen minutes as I rode onward and the dawn lit the sky with pink steel and the road showed as good black top.

Now the real Russia. Pale green fields stretched to the dark green forest, unbroken as far as the eye could see. Hills steep then swooping and climbing in and out of valleys with the country stretching on forever.

DOPE IN THE DARK

I rode on with joy, arriving in Voronezh, a city of almost a million souls, at nearly five in the morning.

The city has wide boulevards with leafy green trees softening the concrete. In the early morning quiet, with no traffic or people, it was a pleasure to ride through. Ms NDrive had decided to play nice for once and I found the address, well the Sat Nav said I'd arrived, but all I could actually see was a brand-new shopping mall with a metre-deep hole by the entrance, into which a car had fallen nose first, and a Sixties style Khrushchev apartment block.

The entrance to the apartment was in a block hidden in a courtyard. Once in the courtyard I was surrounded by more apartment blocks, none of which had the address I'd been given, or any address at all that I could see.

It's not easy differentiating these blocks. My favourite Soviet film has the story of a man who gets drunk on his wedding eve and is sent to the wrong city by his friends. On arrival at the airport, and still a bit tipsy, he asks a taxi driver to take him to his normal address. The driver drops him and our hero enters the block, goes to the apartment and uses his key to get in. The furniture is exactly the same but in a slightly different position.

He gets into bed, falls asleep and is found by a woman... who wonders who is this man, and what he's doing in her bed. The joke of course, is that in a command economy every building and product is exactly the same and is duplicated in every city.

Back to the early morning and me trying to find the apartment by waking up citizens who became increasingly irate and refusing, for some reason, to speak English at dawn. I looked around for someone to help. At six in the morning there weren't a lot of people but I did meet a man out walking his dog. He didn't know the address either but he checked out his own Sat Nav and pointed to a block known by me to be full of non-English speakers, most of whom were angry.

As with all road trips, if something was to go wrong, it would. And it would probably get worse. Hang in here, it gets worse.

I walked back to the block and searched for the address anew.

I had two phones; one had an English SIM card and the other a Ukrainian SIM. But neither phone would work to speak with Tanya, my host in Voronezh. The previous evening my partner in Kyiv held a three-way conversation. She called Tanya and then related the information back and forth via my English phone.

I couldn't call Kyiv; with the time zone change it was about three a.m. and would have been too cruel to call a business partner and have her be angry too. So I wandered around Voronezh in the cool of early morning jabbering to complete strangers asking if they would call a number for me. Most took off quickly; what would you do if an excited, scruffy and bearded biker approached you speaking in a foreign language? But here, my dog walking chum had returned from his walk and understood enough to phone and speak with Tanya. Job done, she'd be down in a moment to find me and he left. Thankfully, I think.

A few moments later an exterior steel door groaned open and out popped the most beautiful little fairy I have ever seen. Even at six a.m. and straight from her bed, Tanya was as pretty as a picture, bubbling with enthusiasm. She hustled me up the stairs to her apartment and dragged all her flatmates out of bed to meet me to. Dmitry, her boyfriend, startlingly handsome with a high cheeked boned face that is a defining feature of many Russians; the third occupant, Rita, as tall and slim as Tanya was short and curved. Rita also greeted me, I am pleased to say, in perfect English.

Tanya and Dima are graduates in journalism, filling in time writing content for a Russian version of eBay. Rita had just graduated with an Economics degree. Much more important though, I was to learn Dima, Rita and her boyfriend Mitka were together in a contemporary jazz band called Alien.

Tanya had cooked a meal the previous evening to greet me with. This was served up and we all sat there at six in the morning talking up a storm about motorcycles, politics, culture, history, education, food and English tea. And, of course, their aspirations for the future. It was from them that I first learned of the deep distrust amongst young and educated Russians of their political system, Moscow in general, and especially President Putin.

Their parents had voted for 'stability', the campaign message endlessly repeated by Putin. Stability for people over forty was a euphemism for not returning to the days of Perestroika that savaged the country economically.

The young people feel despair though. Perestroika was back in their childhood; they didn't know about the Soviet Union or the security of jobs for life. They look at the wealth of Moscow in relation to their own low living standards and feel, with the President now in power for twelve more years, that nothing will change the self-enrichment of the politicians - the rape of their country's wealth continues.

I also discovered the modern young Russian's distrust of America stems from being taught that America only came to the aid of Russia in the war because they, the Americans, could make money from it. They believe that America sat on the side-lines and did nothing until they saw who was going to win and thought they could make money from it. Dima even said that he was taught that America originally financed the Nazi Party.

As an Englishman, I thought this to be far from my learned version of this truth; I was truly astonished to find this alternative version of events.

These revelations aside it was decided we go to Dima's parent's dacha in the evening, so I was shown my couch and everyone went back to sleep for a couple of hours.

Early evening, we set off through the city with Dima leading. Rita had visited her parents whilst the rest of us were sleeping and we picked her up on the way; she rode pillion on my bike.

By the time we got to the countryside dacha it was dark. The lane had deteriorated quickly to a single mud and shingle track sunk deep in the grass; it was two metres wide with ruts between ten and thirty centimetres deep. I'm not too keen on off road at the best of times but with the bike still fully packed and weighing two hundred and eighty kilos plus the passenger it was an interesting, not to say terrifying, ride in the pitch black of night.

Some local residents had blockaded some of the tracks to keep out unwanted visitors and at one point Dima was lost. The girls got off the bikes and Dima rode off on reconnaissance before returning to say he had found a route through, but suggested the girls walked the five hundred or so metres and we two would ride.

My heart sank at the thought of negotiating more of the track but I gathered my courage and followed him on a roundabout route for two kilometres. To get around the barriers he had made a new track through waist high grass – the bumps and ruts couldn't be seen until you'd ridden over them.

The final kilometre was not good; back in a flint and shingle rutted track with u-bends and ten percent drop. When he suddenly turned right and off the track and left me looking at a steep bank of black.

Fortunately, this turn was into the dacha itself. No more. I couldn't do the turn. But with the lane blocked off a further fifty metres hence and no traffic expected that night, with fear riven gratitude I climbed off the saddle to put the bike on the stand and listened to the silence eternal; the sky black and bejewelled with stars.

I said some quick prayers of thanks, one to God for keeping me safe, the other to Dima for giving me the courage to ride off-road in the darkness.

Dima said it wasn't that brave; first he was stoned and had no fear, and he'd fallen off when reconnoitring earlier, but it hadn't hurt too much.

The dacha had no running water, electricity or internet.

Water was drawn from a spring a few hundred metres distant. We walked there in the dark.

I wasn't expecting the ritual of bathing at the spring. The first filled bottles to be emptied over the water carriers who then had to remove all clothing and dance in the flowing water.

Aaaah, The joy of youth, the sadness of older age.

On our return to the dacha cooking was done over an open fire: this evening, tea was made using leaves from bushes and boiled in an ancient blackened pot, potatoes were thrust into the charcoaled wood and mushrooms cooked in a wrapper of aluminium foil.

As a good traveller, I had my pot of Marmite with me; if you're British you'll know it's distinct salt flavour.

Marmite was tried with potatoes and blinis and pronounced to be good even when everyone knows you must be weaned on Marmite to enjoy it as an adult.

Mitka, who had arrived earlier by bus, brought his guitar with him. He played, Rita and Tanya sang and Dima extemporised vocally. Fabulous voices and gifted guitar.

The four friends smoked using tobacco from plants carefully nurtured. It seemed to make them smile more than a standard factory made Marlboro.

But in no time at all the dawn painted the forest in shades of grey; two dawns in two days were taking their toll and I retired to sleep.

The next morning my energetic hosts took me off to the lake, just five hundred metres through the forest to a wide-open clearing with clear pure water. No longer keen on swimming even in my native land I was sufficiently inspired to take a plunge; cold, but invigorating.

After swimming, we had to replenish the drinking water; off we all went to the spring for more nudity and sport. Although I retired from any sport.

On the way, wild strawberries and other berries were plentiful. Having been shown what was edible I joined in the feast from the fields and hedgerow.

I didn't want to make the ride across the flinted tracks in darkness again so Dima and Tanya agreed to return with me to their apartment in Voronezh. Rita was staying on at the dacha with Mitka so riding the tracks without the weight and in daylight was more easily done and the ride back to the city was simple; I just had to follow Dima.

Voronezh in daylight is a Russian standard city. Endless identical apartment blocks, brand new shopping malls and roads chock full of old Ladas and new SUVs of the rich, with little in between. The middle classes, here in 2012, are still emergent.

Upside is that fuel and food is cheap. Good thing about the fuel because it's an enormous country, although people don't travel much. During the years of the command economy few people had cars, most travelled by overnight train.

It was not easy to relocate; especially from a small city to a larger one. A special service was invented to keep people living in small cities, 'propiska' – registration.

Neither was it easy to change this registration, only a very few reasons qualified; all this kept people tied down to their home. Indeed, until 1974 villagers in the countryside did not have passports at all.

This history goes some of the way to explain why Russians with money are more likely to travel abroad than within their own country.

Because there were few cars there was little travel on the roads and little demand for hotels between the cities. This remained the same until the new millennium when loans were more easily obtained to buy new vehicles.

Also, unless it was the coast, every city looked the same; meantime service is everywhere awful, and the roads are generally appalling.

It's changed a bit in the last few years; petrol stations expand across the country although interestingly the state oil company Lukoil still owns more outlets in America than it does in Russia.

The next morning the good fairy Tanya took me to a phone shop where she bought and signed for a Russian SIM card and illegally gave it me.

In the Russian Federation, you must show a passport when you buy a sim card so that the authorities can you track you.

Illegal sim tested to be working and I follow Tanya and Dima on their bike to the city limits where they put me on the road to ride further east. With a wave and kisses thrown and blown they were off.

Alone, I looked east at the arrow straight road as it carved through deep green unbroken forest as far as the eye could see.

Onward then, stiffen the spine, eight hundred kilometres to Samara to join the Trans -Siberian highway.

Recommended
by Hookers

I'm not entirely cavalier about taking long international rides. I had looked at the route to Mongolia on the monitor screen in my office. The screen is forty centimetres wide so the length of the road was reasonable. On a laptop or a tablet, it doesn't look quite so far.

But from the western border of the Russian Federation to its eastern border on the Pacific it's twenty-four centimetres on a landscape page layout. That translates to the reality of twelve thousand kilometres as the crow flies. It's the largest country in the world.

Here in the west the people are still predominantly Caucasian. When I get to the Urals, a thousand kilometres hence, that will change.

The ride right now is not too hard, but my stomach is loose. Luckily my hindquarters

103

were not eaten by marauding bears when I was forced to stop the bike and run into the forest. Twice. And that is enough of that.

But as a side note, one of the mandatory things a traveller should pack is roll of quality toilet paper.

In Ukraine, I'd visited a giant paper factory south west of Kyiv that sucks water from the River Dnieper and discharges frothy dross a bit further downstream.

The factory supplies low quality dun coloured toilet paper for most of Ukraine, and in the days of the Soviet Union distributed it to the lucky few in the cities.

Believe me, better to bring some soft white double layered paper with you. And in the forest, pine needles don't help.

The forest has changed too. Gone are the broad-leafed deciduous oaks. Now it's pine and thin white birch.

The roads are generally quiet; there is not a great deal of commercial traffic on this stretch and time passes pleasantly until the outskirts of the next city.

I am to visit this city twice, but the next visit is several weeks and thousands of kilometres in the future.

On the outskirts, at the cocktail hour, traffic has built up. Actually, it's very congested, nothing is moving and I'm choking on fumes from old Ladas, Volgas, Zils and enormous diesel trucks.

Enough. The ring road is four lanes, overtaking is suicide and legal or illegal I'm filtering in the inside space and when necessary onto the pedestrian free pavements.

I'm looking for somewhere to stay as it's now getting towards seven o clock and I'm loathe to try to find somewhere in the countryside in the ill lit night.

In Russia, to speak English, it's best to ask a woman below the age of forty. This is because Russian men, unless they are working in IT, have no need for English. But women, more curious and some looking for husbands from the West, try to speak and understand English.

So I stop to speak with an attractive young woman and ask for the nearest sleeperie.

She's a hooker of course; why would any young woman saunter casually along the ring road perimeter, but she's pleased it's her mind not her body I'm after. With pleasant, well-spoken English she directs me to a truck stop with a motel attached. She knew about nearby motels.

A kilometre on and I'm turning into the designated truck stop of grey concrete and white wooden beach style cabins with tiny verandas. Huge trailers, ubiquitous white vans and truckers, the latter big, and to my eyes overweight, but they are sons of the road, and friendly; they know of the dangers we face.

Inside and a conversation in broken English with a woman, under forty.

Her standard floral pinafore and pink jowls, not generally to my taste, obviates everything but a single room on my own.

Money is handed over, no credit cards here, and I'm directed with key in hand to a box in which even standing upright is an acquired skill.

The luggage off the bike and into the room. I must vault to get onto the thin mattressed bed. How sizeable truckers manage this feat is unknown. I guess practice, and lack of customer service complaint departments, makes perfect.

But I am safely ensconced and back to the canteen; it couldn't be called a restaurant, for Big Eats.

Big Eats are denied. Most of what I can see is deep fried in batter with no clue to its constituent parts. I point to something that could be soup, fries because I know what they are and bread because it doesn't usually hold poison.

To a table and big men smiling, hands shaken and me with a mouthful answering question as to why I'm crazy enough to be on a motorcycle in this country. And English.

The meal eaten, a stroll around the lorry park for digestion and to bed because I want to be out of the city, early.

As sleep overcomes I hear the mournful wail of the night train, the distant chatter of the points and think, is that the fabled Trans-Siberian?

The morning is bright, the trains, Trans-Siberian or not, no longer disturbing. Luggage affixed, coffee drunk and a pastry eaten, it's still just six a.m. and I'm off with good heart to see what the day will hold.

Trans-Siberian Highway

I crossed the Volga on a long road bridge from Saratov to Engels and thence into a forest eternally green, sparsely populated with small grey concrete and sometimes black wood villages strung along the roadside, thankfully with petrol stations plentiful and the road black tarred. With humps.

I learned later that Samara was first settled in the late fifteenth century and is the sixth largest city of 'All The Russias', sitting prettily at the side of a loop of the massive Volga River.

Pretty it is, but I have not time to tarry for here, after five hours of riding, and after a lunch of Snickers and Pepsi I finally join the Trans-Siberian highway.

Onward then, with fourteen hours of available daylight left to complete the day's target of nine hundred kilometres to Ufa, the Ural Mountains and the beginning of Siberia.

The Trans-Siberian Highway, wide-lane blacktop of my imagination, did not quite live up to expectation. It is, in fact, a loose conglomeration of roads joined by name only, stretching from Moscow to Vladivostok. True, there had been much new building east of Lake Baikal finally providing an almost single route; but here, at my entrance to the highway it was sometimes dual, but mainly a single carriageway chock full of continuous convoys of giant trucks.

Most of the time it was too dangerous to overtake. The oncoming traffic was also in convoys; the road bed had melted in the summer sun, cracked in the winter ice and was churned and rutted deep from the weight of the trucks.

It was safe in the near-side rut, but slow. To overtake, two thirty-centimetre high ridges had to be ridden and then, in the offside rut of the oncoming traffic space to be seen and five, six or seven articulated trucks to be ridden past fast before space was found to tuck back inside to safety. Notwithstanding the vehicle previously hidden on the wrong side of the road now appearing and gunning towards me.

As I rode I mentally wrote a new book of riding instructions to stay safe in Russia.

"Constant focus." I wrote in my head. "Stay alert always, allow distance in front to see forward and overtake only with great caution."

To find myself, moments later, gunning in my helmet from slow speed boredom and screaming operatic overtures at the top of my voice.

Fourteen hours in the saddle, but daylight still, and I've made the day's objective.

SLEEPING IN A NIGHTCLUB

Ufa, where, having had no luck searching for a couch I'm now searching for a cheap hotel. The first I found was just too awful even for me; I carried on looking until, tiring fast, I found a nightclub with rooms attached at the side.

I didn't discover it was a night club until noise in the night woke me up; but hey, who am I to complain for twenty bucks and breakfast thrown in for free.

I parked as close to reception as I could, three stories of glass frontage arranged for me to look at my reflection as a proper and proud Adventure Rider, but seeing instead the figure of a saddle tramp, grimy from head to foot, pink jacket turned to black.

To reception where, for this is Russia, I paid for the room in advance. Outside to find two security men insisting I moved the bike. I thought, at the beginning, they were demonstrating their authority but later realised they were protecting the bike from Clubbers with cameras to sit on for selfies.

However, the men could see I was struggling – my ribs were complaining from the jouncing and jostling of the road – so they helped me to carry my luggage up to my room.

I was grateful, and tired and asleep by eleven but up at twelve because of the noise. I walked around outside not enjoying either the crowds or the music, smoked a cigarette with no added additives and went back to bed.

In this morning, no helpmates so the luggage carried alone to the bike to discover, at breakfast of cucumber and cold cuts that Ms NDrive had limbered up over-night to give early morning navigation a good kick in the teeth.

The one page A4 portrait printed map of Russia was of no use either to guide me out of the city. Two guys in a car, reading my license plate that said I was from out of country, not just out of town and reading also the consternation on my face, asked, in English, if they could help.

I said "Yes, I'm looking for the Trans-Siberian Highway, heading east."

Then I'm chasing through the city's rush hour, heart pounding, following the little green Lada with all the high-speed skills I can muster. Twenty minutes and they're turning off and away, waving me forward to the road to the East.

SIBERIA BEGINS

In the mountains, the next morning, kindness is extended by a family of three. At a petrol stop in the cool of the pine forest I am sitting on the kerb next to the bike when the family arrives, spreads a blanket to sit and allow their baby to stretch and crawl. They offer me food, gladly accepted, of tomato and cheese and bread and sweet black chai. Sergey, his wife Valentina and baby Alex, the latter gurgling, the former chatting in limited English about life in Siberia and the tentacles of political corruption everywhere. Why do people talk this way to strangers? Perhaps the old life of neighbours informing on incorrect conversation is starting again. Good to find a stranger, tell of their truth and have him express it more widely in the west.

Whatever the motivation I took sweet pleasure from these people in a clearing in the forest in the mountains of the Urals.

Two hours of more climb later and then it's all downhill, out of the mountains into Siberia, the true beginning of Central Asia, seeking the city of Chelyabinsk.

This is the third time I've circumnavigated Tank Town.

The hotel I'm looking for, according to Ms NDrive, is thirty metres in front of me, is simply not there. I've parked twice, walked around, even asked a couple of people who simply shook their heads and walked away. One pointed, but in retrospect I think he simply wanted to get rid of a biker speaking foreign.

So now in a narrow side street I attempt a three-point turn and with a car to my left appearing from nowhere leaving me hot, sweaty and reclining in the road with the bike on top of me.

Pain swells outward from my ribs and I'm eternally grateful to a passerby and the car driver who lift the bike, and me, to a more normal and vertical position.

No damage to the bike, but much to me, and I'm losing the end of my tether. But who to blame? I got myself here and into this mess and there's no starship around to carry me off to a life of ease and comfort.

Astride my motorcycle with expletives leaking from my lips and I'm onto the pavement at a speed slow enough to read the building numbers.

Aaah. The hotel. Hidden around this corner with no flashing light or advertisement saying come, sleep here.

Parked, in through the door barely able to walk, to negotiate with the black skirted and not attractive night time receptionist.

No flirting or smiles to assist the transition from motorcyclist to much wanted guest. A ruinous expense calculated, payment upfront and in cash; negotiations not considered, and I am instructed to park the bike in the security yard out back.

There is nothing wrong with where I am I think, but here I can see that the rules are the rules.

In pain, I ride to the yard. There are no security gates or guards but an overhead light blinks on and off and on and off.

To reception again, and I try to explain, through admittedly a very poor mime, that ribs are sundered, the security is not secure and I wish to get my luggage inside and into my room. With assistance, could you kindly provide?

Nyet was understandable in any language.

Exhausted, adrenaline depleted, breathing in gasps I retrieve my luggage, two side, one top and a tank bag and a helmet.

In reception again and by happenstance an internal security guard is hanging around doing nothing that I can see. I politely ask, quite possibly plead, and even offer money for help to get the kit to my room.

There is shouting; he actually and severally stamps his foot in anger before walking away. Ex-Soviet Customer Service does not change.

There is no lift in this establishment. In three trips I get everything up to the corridor of the first floor, find a couch, say "Fuck it." and lay down to sleep.

I am shaken awake by another and older and equally hard faced woman also dressed in black; she is the mistress of this floor.

She points, pointedly, down the corridor. The corridor is green, very long and ill-lit. I shake my head, point to my ribs, the bags.

She leaves, returning forthwith with a trolley normally used to convey tea, in the mornings, to guests. Who have presumably paid for the privilege in advance whether it arrives or not.

Cases on the trolley, me gasping and pushing and following on behind. At the corridor's end a left turn, more steps with no handrail and a massive iron door. With two hands and some muscle she swings open the door, points to a room and leaves with her nose in the air.

I am not too pleased with this arrangement but managed to get the cases up the stairs one by one and into the room. Where there was room for the cases but not really for me and a bed.

The bathroom was communal. I'm glad this is a four-star hotel, not somewhere cheap and nasty.

Laying down to ease my battered body and just as I relax my phone, with its illegal Russian sim-card, begins to ring.

In my pain and frustration, I had forgotten a meeting, arranged some time ago, with an architect to take dinner and views of the city.

"Ten minutes." I manage to say. To the communal ablutions and rust flavoured water from out of the rose, more pain killers and I'm down the stairs to the street and being given hugs which I have to take gently and with care.

Nadia and boyfriend, couch-surfing chums, bringing an oasis of calm friendship to my self-generated storm. We walk, slowly, on one of the few remaining streets that has the original wooden homes built a century before.

Then to the Wall Street café. named by its owner in an expression of pique and minor revolution.

Coffee, strong, and my friends with beer, I recounted the tale of the hotel from Hell.

"Ahh," they said. "Security guards. Everywhere here they use the excuse, even when they have nothing to do, of protecting the building and will never help out."

We talk, then, of Tank Town; it's origin and how its soubriquet was earned.

In the last years of the nineteenth century, they explained, a man was charged by Peter the Great to open up Siberia. So in fine Russian tradition, that of copying the West instead of original thinking, a railway to start the roll.

The first was built from Moscow, over the Urals and into this city. And from here, at the same time, the Trans-Siberian Railway built forward as a gateway to Siberian settlement.

The town, by then a hundred and fifty years old, expanded with the immigrants. Fully fifteen percent of Russia's then population passed through here for the east.

More. With German forces advancing in World War II Stalin ordered that the factories of war should be hidden east of the Urals. Not surprising then, with a railhead to hand, that to Chelyabinsk came the manufacture of tanks, ammunition and later, rockets and missiles. And known from then on as Tank Town.

My companions were clever and well educated. Nadia, the architect, her man in IT, both under thirty. They'd hoped to start their own business, but now, frustrated, they wanted to move to the west.

"To start a business here," said Nadia, "you need all the normal things. Capital, talent, enthusiasm and more than a little courage."

But there's more. Before you can start a legitimate business, there is documentation. A lot. Legions of civil servants to be paid, under the table, for permissions to trade. Then, when all is settled the trip to the Mayoral offices where the truth is explained.

You have jumped all the hurdles, paid all the bribes. But now you must sign to allow ten percent of the value of your sales, forever, to go direct to the Mayor as a political contribution. Who deducts a small fee and sends it onward to the Party and evidently to the President too.

On top of this there is even more tax. On profits and employees for which you are made permanently and personally responsible. In the countries of the former Soviet Union they have missed one of capitalism's tenents. Under capitalism, as known in the West, what goes up can also come down. In these eastern countries, no matter what the trading situation, the tax and other officials will not accept that a company can ever go broke. There is no limited liability; once started, it seems you're in it for life. Unless of course you're an Oligarch. And then it doesn't count.

Small corruption is endemic, just a way of life. But the mandatory and illegal political contribution is a tax too far for my friends.

Especially as they hate the man at the top of the tree who champions the Church and equally illiberal causes and starts wars to redirect the populace from concerns and problems internal. Not to mention enriching himself.

My friends, their friends and friends of their friends are all under thirty. Talented. Bright. They all hope to go to the West. If not, they'll all go to waste.

Of note. Eight months later, in February 2013, a meteor weighing eleven thousand tonnes exploded twenty-five kilometres above the mountains behind the city with a force some thirty times greater than that of the atomic bomb dropped on Hiroshima. Of injuries there were many, but no deaths were reported.

CAPITAL OF OIL

I'd arrived here for three reasons.

One, I'm told the highway from Chelyabinsk to Omsk is truly bad and long; it demanded a stop halfway.

Second, Tyumen was the only place in between the aforesaid destinations.

And third, Irving Berlin was born here in the city. But of him I found not a thing.

There was a turf war here, four centuries or so ago. The Tyumenese claimed the honour of being the first township in all Siberia. The indigenous peoples didn't agree.

I knew only that the land had been stolen from Tartars of true Siberian descent. At more or less the same time and in much the same way other, non-Russian Europeans, stole America from the tribes who lived there first. My own country, of course, at the forefront of pillage, rape and native re-education.

I am greeted by the father of the young man I have come to see. He is not tall, the father, about my age but looking, I think, older, wearing slippers, black trousers and an old facsimile fair-isle jumper. He smiles proudly and displays a mouthful of gold, the absolute apex of Siberian dental skill.

Cases unloaded, into a lift that works, and to the apartment where I meet the mother in a headscarf as a fashion point; no veil needed in a city of the Orthodox Church. Their daughter, sub-teen, black eyes and mouth showing shiny white teeth wide open, openly staring at the first live man from the west that she's ever met.

I am welcomed, sat down and offered black tea from a bowl with no handles. The culture has changed for this, albeit Siberia, is central Asia too.

Tyumen is the oil capital of the Russian Federation, but there is no oil. There is in Kazakhstan in the south and in oil and gas fields four hundred kilometres north, shipped both ways on the wide river Tura in steamboats; the first of which in Russia, was built right here.

Ilkumen, my couch-surfing host had arrived and takes me first to secure the motorcycle. I'd rather he hadn't for it stood quite nicely, covered and locked, in the carpark next his block apartment building. But like everyone here he was afraid of theft, and particularly on behalf of his new friend from the west.

So, I had to mount the motorcycle and follow him slowly over rough open ground, deep and dangerous ruts and bumps and into purportedly secure parking. Security meant there were lights on at night and guarded by a guard who would anyway sleep and to whom an outrageous five euros were slipped.

A stroll to the city itself, where, amongst more dreary and identical apartment blocks softened by trees, were found handsome Civic buildings, an Opera

House and, more interestingly to my eyes at least, a much greater abundance of neat clean streets of one storey traditional wooden houses, most blackened with age, some painted white and pale blue, and all with carefully hand carved weather boarding, tiles and filigree panels.

I was pleasantly surprised, for there are few places in the Russias, apart from empty villages deep in the country, where traditional wooden houses survive.

One reason it seems, that there is little historical building east of Poland, is that most buildings built in the past were made from wood from the forest and simply rotted away. Russians themselves, like much of the New World inhabitants too, are not generally atavistic and build over the old as soon as they can. Bigger, brighter, baubled.

Return to the apartment and his sister has changed her clothes to impress in jet black, sewn with much splendid shiny silver. And pleased that she'd taken the trouble, smiling with less nerves in the now.

We eat, a kind of Nasi Goreng but not with a name that I can write or pronounce and the father is off to the bath house and sauna as there is no hot water in the block and hasn't been for weeks.

I talk with my host who is studying to be a doctor. He knows that once he graduates here he has another four years more hard studying to complete. For in the West, where he's going, these qualifications won't pass muster. And needs to have English, spoken like a native.

To sleep on a couch upholstered in tan with gold and jewels twinkling and then up in the morning early with a breakfast of salami and cheese and lemon juiced chai.

Once rescued from security, no guard to be seen, I'm on the bike on a good road heading east toward somewhere called Kurga.

But before we leave Oil City an agrarian item of note.

On river worn cliffs high to the east of the city, there appeared to be a concentration of invisible and soundless animals, the like of which I'd never seen or heard.

By the ripe smell, there must be thousands of the odiferous beasts.

For a motorcyclist, when travelling, such fragrance is not always a joy. In this case, the foulness was omnipresent and had me gagging in my helmet even with the wind in my face.

It transpired that here in the countryside of Tyumen was the largest butter production company in the country.

But of the cattle, I saw none.

ROCKET ARMY

The road was not as advertised. It was good, black and fast, the only downside being the tar that was sprayed over my proud red wax jacket. Now black on the front and in creases.

The steppe seemed endless, the only movement a trick of the eye in passing. The forest moved closer, and then backed away where trees had been felled in the past when the land was ploughed and thickly sown with wheat.

In truth, there seemed little cultivation going on at all.

I knew that Siberia, once Russia's bread basket, had a dramatic crop failure around fifteen years ago, leading to the mass abandonment of villages and a tide of people moving to the cities.

Government, of any stripe, always thinks it knows best. These lands had been badly managed since the Russian Revolution. Because the land was wide and never ending, crop rotation was never considered. Eventually it fell infertile and erosion ruined a lot. Country people stopped breeding, fewer to work the land; many moved to the cities, cheaper to import food than grow it.

Khrushchev had a go in the '60s. He sent more than half a million volunteer students into the back of beyond with instructions to grow more and varied food. For a while it worked, but the workers in the cities disliked the new food not made from corn. And soil erosion returned to ruin the rest of the effort.

So here, on the steppe, there were side roads winding to villages standing empty, some signed, most not.

The most remarkable effect was the emptiness at cross roads. Throughout Ukraine and most of European Russia the cross roads were usually busy with babushkas selling seasonal fruit and vegetables by, literally, the old tin bucket full.

Here, on the Trans-Siberian Highway in the Central Asian section, the sun shone and the wind blew and the crossroads were steadfastly empty.

There was some activity, though nothing that I liked.

Sixty kilometres short of Omsk in the wide-open spaces of nothing, clouds gathered fast and two searing bolts of lightning conjoined and crashed and produced a searing ball of light directly in front of my eyes.

The crash of thunder and air pressure pressed me hard down in the saddle and thick rain splashed down to limit visibility, in moments, to a just a few metres ahead.

Water flowed in the road like a river; mud sluiced from the edge and the whole turned into a bombsite.

I had no choice, no cover, and rode on, slowly, into the storm. In a terrifying ten minutes it was over; Nature's violence depleted then expended. Then the road got worse and the rain came back.

I'd always wanted to visit the city of Omsk.

Forty years or more before, when I'd sat in the driving seat of a missile submarine, it was one of the targets listed, or so I believed at the time.

And then later, reading a book about spies, the fictitious account told of silos and missiles pointed west. Or in this case, as Omsk is central, probably pointed to cities of the U.S.A.

Here and there were clues; sparse it's true, but the military had a definite presence.

They were originally called the Rocket Army but more precisely and today it's the Lenin Red Banner Missile Division under command of the 33rd Army. The missiles in both silos and mobile too, to confuse.

Omsk is not the place for too much friendly conversation and enquiry. I left quietly, and early, in the morning of the very next day.

DEAD CENTRE

The lack of rural population affects we travellers too.

Mr Putin made a joke, reported around the world. He was being heckled, at an economics conference by a brave man from Siberia who said, "The cities may be wonderful, but where I'm from, in Siberia, I cannot afford a car." Mr Putin said, allegedly, "Why would you want a car when there are no roads?"

A very bad joke for the spokesman from Siberia but there was no humour in the truth.

This road, the Highway, on which I'm travelling now has lost all trace of anything in concrete or tarred black macadam. Deep ruts dug by trucks when the economy was good, old tar that had melted in the sun's fierce heat and then later cracked asunder by winter's grip, verges that merged into grassland and no longer any road marks as the road itself could hardly even be seen.

Parked next to a closed down petrol station I have, by endless and desperate calculation, seventy-five kilometres of petrol left.

No, I have not yet bought a jerry can to supplement the tank. But I will try, too late, in a couple of thousand kilometres from here.

Fifty kilometres onward and another deserted outlet for fuel. I ride on until I pass a sign that says бензин, benzene, at its best. Fifty kilometres hence.

The fuel light warning is glowing yellow on my dash. So I turn and return to a deserted place that I passed a little way back.

The trouble has been that the land becomes more lawless the further east I ride. There are petrol stations like small oases; but none show lights, or welcome windows or signs of oil or ice-cream.

They stand, these petrol stations, at the roadside forlorn and uniformly rusty from sheet steel welded on all four sides with a single pump in the courtyard.

I stand too, perplexed, motorcycle at the pump waiting for its feed, looking at the building clad seven metres high in thick sheets of steel

With loud bang, a small rectangular drawer has opened in the steel. It is at chest height so I am obliged to bend, to supplicate, and then try looking inside.

A voice from within, "Skolka?" because here you pay up front.

And meaning "How much benzene do you want, in money?" How the hell would I know? I just want to fill it up.

A calculation. It costs fifteen pounds to fill the tank on my small and expensive Island. Here, petrol is half the cost. So, say seven pounds and fifty pence. To roubles, five hundred and fifty. To my wallet, only six hundred in currency and no cards accepted here

I lay the money in the drawer and the pump starts to whir. Running, in case the pump power fails, I put the nozzle in the tank and press as hard as I can, noting only now that the strength is 92 and I should be using 98.

The last drips into the tank, closed, secured and nozzle shoved into the holster.

The drawer, in the wall, is being rattled loudly. I walk back and see there is change, in coins, being offered to me. A surprise for me and give a grateful "Thank you." with a grunt returned and heard from the bowels of the all steel building.

Onward until I was lost, relatively speaking, on the outskirts of a small grey city.

The city viewed at sunset, which in these parts is ten in the night, and I'm stabbing the phone for Sat Nav clues. I find a route and set forward riding, feeling something brush pass as I go. Five hundred metres and the phone is no longer on show.

I walk back down the track and find the phone leaking light in the pitch dark that now surrounds me.

To the motorcycle waiting and I can't find the keys. On hands and knees and near tears of frustration and anger at self, now crawling all the way back to where I'd found the phone and keys recovered safely.

Deep breath, praise to all gods and castigation to the fool who had lost them and I'm back on the bike and into the town and the Sat Nav fails, completely.

I did what I often did in such circumstances; stopped at a lit-up petrol station, plentiful in the city, and waited for a biker. Quite soon a large customised Ural throbbed into sight, the rider in standard black leather and his girl, on the back, in a standard tiny skirt and high boots.

I approached with a hand outstretched for shaking, wearing my widest smile and all the while waving a piece of paper like a white flag of surrender. Both smiled back and, haltingly, I explained that written on the paper was the place I needed to go.

"Of course, one moment please." he said in perfect English. He filled his tank, paid and suggested we have a smoke before moving off. So that we did, whilst he welcomed me and enquired to the nature of my visit. I said, slowly and in perfectly enunciated BBC English, "I am here to find out if Siberian bears shit in the woods."

He looked at me with a broad smile breaking across his face. "Not in Siberia. They have nothing to eat". Naturally this led to vodka and accommodation being offered, both of which I had to decline. After more laughter, conversation and finally, a hug not dissimilar to said bears, he jumped on his bike with his girl perched correctly and shouted, "Follow me." Easier said than done as we roared across the city avoiding potholes the size of small cars, skittering across tramlines and ignoring red lights. With my heart repositioned in my throat we pulled up twenty minutes later outside a standard, drab, Khrushchev issue apartment block. "In there." he shouted over the engine noise. "Good luck English."

The night quietened with their departure. I pulled myself out of the saddle, took my go-bag out of top box and threw a camouflaged cover over the bike. A little incongruous in the city, but hidden from the eyes of the casually dishonest. To the door of the apartment building, buzzing of bells and there, in pyjamas, stood one of two of my newest new friends.

It was late, work to be done on the morrow and after a bowl of borscht, some bread, tea and light conversation, I was shown to my bed on the kitchen floor – a mattress most thoughtfully provided by my charming hostesses; both of whom were lucky to be alive and not, in the terrible parlance, correctively raped in this homophobic country.

They had little problem in our initial chat with sharing their secret loving life with a westerner who was in their lives for two nights only; but to speak of it to family or colleagues could cost them very dear.

Homosexuality is not illegal in Russia, but pressure from the nascent Orthodox Church has politicians queuing up to talk of the "Satanic practice."

Mr Putin absolved himself in a speech about the banning of Gay Pride marches in 2007 and passed the buck to his minions saying *"With regards to what the heads of regions say, I normally try not to comment. I don't think it is my business. My relation to gay parades and sexual minorities in general is simple – it is connected with my official duties and the fact that one of the country's main problems is demographic. But I respect and will continue to respect personal freedom in all its forms, in all its manifestations"*

So Gay Pride marches, which started in Moscow in 2005 are not illegal either; but the local and regional authorities will not allow them to be held in most cities claiming the chances of violent outbreaks are too high.

"Corrective rape", to force gay women to a path of presumed acceptable behaviour is still kept secret here; not spoken about in society. If reported, the Police would ignore it or worse, try more conversions themselves in their cells.

The next day, with my friends at work, I stroll to the town to observe local culture.

Like most Russian cities, it had had a Khrushchev make-over. Endless apartment blocks of identical design, differing only in the placement of trees.

The night before I had trouble with tramlines; in daylight I saw just how many silvered tracks were spread through the cobbled city streets.

Equally, the sheer number of ancient grey and dark red painted trams with a press of people on-board was another great surprise. In Ukraine, only the very poor travel by tram. Not just trams clogged the roads; ageing cars of all brands, omnipresent white mini-buses and myriad assorted vans, horn-honking SUVs of the self-important banged and clattered into potholes all striving to be somewhere else as fast they could crawl.

The lens of my Canon wasn't working, a technical fault of some kind so I'm looking for a camera shop for a while-you-wait repair or at worst, a replacement lens.

After two shops, I was discovering fast that no repairs could be affected, nor a separate lens to be bought either. I could buy a whole new camera, true. But the cost was not to be countenanced so I bought instead a small one that would fit in my pocket; the downside being restrictive resolution; there'd be no big pics for posters or magazine articles.

I thought I would surprise my friends with a light Spanish supper. We all do this, don't we? Try to cook meals from our culture to present to another with nary a hope of gathering the right ingredients. I thought to keep it simple. Melon and Serrano ham. I'd seen melons in abundance in shops and available from roadside vendors. After searching four supermarkets it was apparent that Spanish exporters hadn't got past the Urals, so I thought I'd just go for the melon.

This roadside vendor, short dark and probably from a former Soviet Republic three thousand kilometres to the south, called out "Ripe melons!" with a smile under the bright nylon striped awnings of his temporary stall.

But his call was in a language that I did not understand so he may well have been shouting "Look at this fool!".

To the stall then, looking but not touching the ripe golden fruit. And then, because I had found no ham, switching abruptly to the green, chosen by size, not taste.

I offered my wallet, he took out some paper and gave coins in return. Happy with my prize it took two more days to discover I'd paid ten dollars for a fifty-cent fruit.

The melon was eaten, shared between three and for more entertainment, having talked about opera, the girls decided to take me to the town and a bar at the Opera House. The Opera House itself, being high summer, was closed.

In the bar, another surprise; an introduction to a strikingly attractive woman, the Prima Donna Soprano from the Opera company. I will confess that although I love opera I am not particularly knowledgeable. I learned much, but regrettably heard no arias in private performance.

We talk about work. Veronica is an architect, revising drawings and mostly seeking new permissions to build. Margheritte meanwhile is the finance Director of a Construction company. I thought not of collusion, more of joint interests.

Afterward, we strolled through the town to look at an unprepossessing little white church protected by tramlines centred in the middle of a roundabout. This, they told me, was the exact centre of 'All The Russias.' And whilst I stood marvelling that I had been riding this country for almost two weeks and had only just got halfway, a minor miracle occurred.

A man, leaning on the pedestrian barrier that fenced off the church, heard us speaking English and introduced himself. In conversation it transpired that, almost fifty years earlier whilst I was sitting in a submarine with missiles pointing at this very city, he too was in a missile boat, all pointing at my home too. It was, for me, an extraordinary moment. Here I stood, shaking the hand of a man who was my exact counterpart separated only by an ideology. For both of us, the miracle of peace was profound.

Change of Plan

The following morning, I had to admit, finally, regretfully and only to myself in private, that I was in too much pain from my unhealed ribs to continue my route to Lake Baikal and Ulaanbaatar, Mongolia's capital city. The roads I travelled were not good; the constant pounding and gyrations giving no relief.

So I left the city and turned right and a bit, to head south east.

On the road, an aside; at another remote and rusting petrol station four hundred kilometres further southeast and I meet a thirty something tall and very wide priest, sporting a crumpled white dog collar and long black beard with two acolytes beside him. The priest, whose name was Alexei, was the leader of the gang. All three were mounted on Ural custom motorcycles. We filled our tanks and under the canopy and over a smoke and shared bottle of vodka,

I had coffee, we chatted about the resurgence of Russia, the end of all wars and Chechnya. It just so happened I'd recently read a biography by a Russian soldier who had been drafted to the Chechen war so I may have even sounded knowledgeable.

The upshot was they wanted to give this 'crazed lone Englishman' a friendship gift. A search was made and one of the acolytes came up with a spent AK brass cartridge said to have been collected in Chechnya and therefore giving great good luck. A hole had already been drilled in the side of the brass so, with great pride, dignity and not a little shuffling and stumbling we enacted an official transfer from his keyring to mine. The priest blessed me and my bike and I upped and left with undying camaraderie ringing in my ears.

Back on the road, the AH4, part of the Great Asian Highway system which, if I wished, could take me all through

Mongolia to Yarantai, the Chinese border and on, non-stop to Karachi in Pakistan. The road needs some work, as does my mind.

INTO THE VALLEY

A couple of days and further on to Gorno-Altaysk, capital of the Altai Republic. A town of fifty thousand souls featuring a supermarket of poured concrete three storeys high, and a theatre, a museum I did not visit, and a big square with heroes cast in bronze where I'm waving my phone at a woman passing by.

The village I seek is too small to be found on Sat Nav although I feel, or rather hope, it is close by. My host says it is but I've tried to find the road there twice. And failed.

I say to my host on the phone "Shout HELLO very loud." But the woman passing by increases her stride and I find a teen instead. Said teen takes the phone with the confidence of youth, listens and points me forward. "Good luck!" he cries with a smile. In English.

An hour and I was still looking for the house of my host but looked instead at a small, strange, propellered aircraft hidden by trees. A relic perhaps, of previous wars.

The village was in an evergreen steep sided valley winding beside a turquoise river in the rugged Altai mountain range. My host dressed in yellow with her daughter waving energetically at the side of the road and I'm riding down a loose stone track and stop, gratitude welling anew.

Altai means, in both Chinese and Mongolian, gold.

I didn't see gold mines in this beautiful, peaceful place but the mountains shone gold in the sun.

As well as the aircraft I'd seen, perhaps, an Ibex and other small deer, wild boar running the road, heard, I think, a moose but not yet seen the rare snow leopard. Evidently there were bears and wolves in the forest too. And in Barnaul, through which I'd recently passed, a rare Caspian tiger was shot just a couple of years ago. For fun.

I didn't really know, until I'd arrived, that these mountains are the confluence of the borders of Siberia, Kazakhstan, Mongolia and China.

Together different habitats, like the steppe, northern taigas and alpine vegetation come together to create a unique environment; I rode much slower so as not to upset it.

There are many new buildings, back west at the head of the valley, mainly in wood but sometimes built from brick,.

It so happened that President Putin's government had been pouring lineless money into the area to improve tourist facilities so that Russian city dwellers would holiday here at home instead of going to Turkey, the only place in the western world that Russians can easily get visas.

The fear was that if the whole Russian population went on holiday to Turkey they'd discover great food, sensationally cheap accommodation and high level service, thus guaranteeing, on return, dissatisfaction for the rest of their lives.

Although billions had allegedly been officially spent, there didn't seem to be much to show for it until my hostess told me that the reason her village had been split in half by a brand new eight lane blacktop was to convey people from the tiny airport (now enlarging to take jets from Moscow), up into the mountains where a palace had been built for the most important man in Russia, and his mistress. The much-improved road ran only between the airport and the palace; I assumed much of the vaunted billions had stayed in someone's pocket.

Meanwhile, the populace continued to travel to Turkey, had a great time and came home to complain about local conditions.

Until, in the now, because their leader needed another war to stay in power, they can't get visas to anywhere.

Surprising simple pleasures. This was deep Siberia; my hosts owned their three-room wooden cottage but still occasionally had to draw water from the well to cook their home-grown vegetables.

Few flowers grown here; food is much more important. At the end of the carefully tended thirty metre square vegetable garden was the banya; the combined bathing and steam room rightly beloved by Russians. Of note; I am led to believe that Russia's forebears were using banyas a thousand years before Europe got around to a strip wash standing in a bucket.

Here today, fortunately for me, there is no snow to roll around in either.

Two metres further was the outside lavatory that drained into a sump below. Here you can sit daily in style and look through the gaps at mountains rearing high above.

The wood-fired banya was usually shared between husband, wife and their young daughter too. In August I loved it, but in winter in these parts the temperature drops and stays at minus twenty centigrade. You'd need to run down the path pretty quick.

Outside bathroom and not always running water; but in the same cottage I saw my first ever 3D film on TV. A massive TV, full surround sound and Avatar prancing across the screen, speaking well in Russian.

My hostess, Vika, is an English teacher and beautiful with high cheekbones and gold flecked tawny eyes. She's also petite, slim and naturally blonde; lovely, clever and warm-hearted. Her daughter, a minx if ever there was one, has her husband's dark colouring and learns to play and beat me later, the word game Hangman, in her language and in mine.

With Vika's husband at work in the local prison and her daughter to her primary school we had the opportunity to chat all day about life in the East and West.

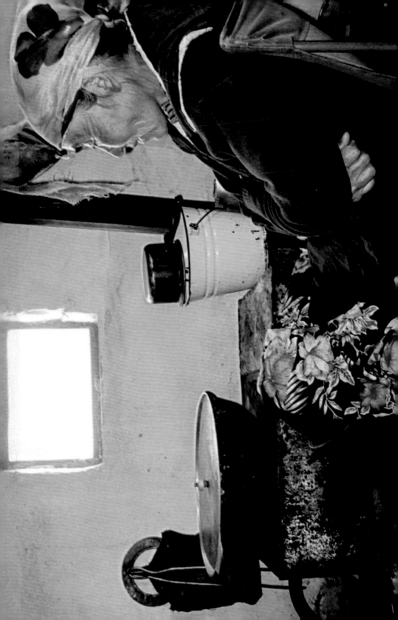

KAZAKHSTAN

KYRGYSTAN · TADJIKISTAN
TURKMENISTAN · UZBEKISTAN

1:3 000 000

~~KRAKOVA~~ may border

POLAND →

A4   toward Tornav (NOT E40)

A4 E40 CRACOW

E40 A4 DRESDEN , (20 miles ⇧ to)

A14   LEIPZIG / MAGDEBURG/K

41.6 miles

A38 to LEIPZIG SUDOST / GOTTINGE

~~A387~~ KASEL A7/E45/

A49 DREIECK KASSEL-SUD

A44 to KREUZ KSWEST PADERB

DORTMUND

E63/A44 (2 miles)

E331/A44 DUISBURG EINDHOVE

E34/ A40 EINDHOVEN

313/E34/AB ANTWERP OOST

A14 Ring Road

E40 BRUGGE OOSTENDE XPO

E40/A18 CALAIS.

Westerners generally are much more open than people in the East; I think she was both surprised and gratified that I would speak openly about feelings, 'women's problems' and everything else under the sun.

Part of which was politics. Listening to Mr Putin's entreaties on the stability of the Nation and promises for raised amounts and payments, on time, of salaries for employees of the State and pensioners too, she'd given him her vote. As had her family but not her husband who thought him a fraud.

A windfall for the family. To build blacktop access to the new built palace of love high up there in the mountains, part of their land had been sold. Six months and a new fence and a road made from stones to their door but no money as yet, still coming.

Dima, the husband, now home from poking food through the bars, asked how to tell his workmates that an English was staying all day alone with his wife. Vika retorting, "Don't tell them." Score one for the newly discovered Altai women's liberation movement.

I'm taken by car on a sightseeing tour.

More turquoise rivers that churn through deep gorges, a road bridge with no road, another bridge, narrow with wooden planks that I would not attempt to ride. Here was a stunning church, with saints' bones interred, built on a tiny island in the river, accessed only by yet another dangerously swaying cracked planked bridge.

The river has real force and is dammed for power in several places. Tourism has just started to touch this far down the valley and there are bars off from the road, neon lit from the river's hydro power, and holiday chalets filled with the sort of Russian visitors who like wooden chalets, vodka, beer, loud music, large bellies and arm wrestling. But, as I said, they're hidden from the road.

Back in the car I see a single camel strolling; surely not a natural member of the local fauna. A four-wheel drive adventure centre, Japanese jeeps painted green; and still in green but brighter hued, a magnificent Ural motorcycle with side car attached, the high points picked out in red. The windows of the wooden home next to which it is parked are painted too in green. And red.

THE BORDER TOWN

Early, and I'm on the road to Ongudaysky with the mountains magnificent in deep green, blue, and peaks, still in Summer, covered deep with snow. At Ortoluk the mountains veer right, slide over the horizon and onto the Gobi Desert; where I am not intending to go.

My nerves are still shot over petrol and the lack of it, so I'm stopping to fill every hundred kilometres. The petrol stations remain remote, welded with steel and the villages, like the petrol, seem to get poorer too.

After the mountains, the Chuyskiy Trakt, a mediocre main road next to the Katun river that flows placidly through a pale olive coloured landscape of low round hills swelling out to the flat of steppe. There no trees, anywhere. Or birds.

To ride on roads cracked and torn through the dusty town Kosh-Agach and arrive the next day in the late afternoon at Tashanta, the border town jump off for Mongolia.

By the time I'd arrived, the border was closed.

The town boasted a café, perhaps thirty prefabricated houses, a small store, petrol station and a barracks for border guard troops. Around it, the steppe with the occasional yurt, dots of white, in the distance.

There also happened to be, a few hundred metres out, five large radar dishes connected and pointed at China just over the horizon. Not welcoming Chinese tourists then. Nyet yet.

The nearest hotel, it transpired, was a hundred kilometres back down the road I had already travelled. It was a road in name only and I had no intention of riding it again.

But here a mini yurt set up as a kind of advertisement and an occasional sleeping place for the young woman who owned the café.

I begged to stay the night and for seven dollars she, or rather her father, who sat in the late evening sun, finally agreed. She was staying in the yurt that evening too; so, to protect her reputation she had another girl arrive as a chaperone.

Physiognomy has changed; there were few Russian or European facial types here. People are broader cheeked, noses flatter, skin darker, eyes with epicanthic folds. But they're Kazakhs, not Mongolians.

Local people and culture; a continuous source of fascination to me.

I'm granted access to the over-nighting yurt. Inside, the complex wooden frame is evident, devoid of decoration. A round table in the centre and two pull-out sofas for beds at the sides.

With cows, mooing as a late night entertainment.

In the morning to the border but I'd misunderstood. Today it was closed for a holiday

Nothing for it but to return to the yurt and the café, beg for a bed and agreed; but tonight to stay on my own for the dark haired brown eyed Yuliya had business in the city back down the road.

In the shop to buy unidentified food, heated in the café's microwave; consumed by me and none the wiser of what I had to eat.

I had been told, by Yuliya, of a toilet.

It stood, solitary and in splendour, overlooking the steppe and the far-off hills, next door to rusty wrecked and decaying military buildings of some kind.

By the smell, it was of a simple dump and drop construction, old wood surrounding a hole in the ground.

Needs must, but an Alsatian guarded the privy. At his growl, a soldier appeared.

"Mozhna toilet pazhalsta?" tripped from lips, surprising even myself.

"Nyet!" said the soldier, and in English, "It is mine."

Again, and pleasantly spoken I thought "I'd really like to use it. I brought my own paper with me."

"Nyet, mine." And the Alsatian growled to agree.

So the toilet remained unused, by me at least at this time. And I stepped carefully down to the steppe, outdoors, alone, with a view of my very own. Wondering at the cost to the Russian Army of a man to guard a lavatory.

I'd sight-seen the village, photographed apparently unwashed children, buildings and shacks, the lavatory, soldiers and most of the denizens too; found the petrol station at the end of the single street, filled up, lost money on the Euro exchange rate and now had nothing more to do.

Supper appeared. Included in the bed rate. Goat perhaps, with rice and a salad of tomato and cucumber.

The border was getting busy. Werner, on a bicycle from Germany, arrived and disclosed his budget was tighter than mine when he put up his tent. For free.

In the night on my couch listening to the singing of slightly drunken soldiers getting closer to the yurt and then loud rattling on the door and voices crying "Dyvozhka, Dyvozhka." They were searching for the women, who anticipating the holiday party had already, earlier and wisely, left and gone to the town.

The cyclist, annoyed with noise, Teutonic, braver and bigger than me stepped out of his tent and said clearly in English for all to hear "Fuck off. Now."

And, fortunately, the soldiers did, and left us alone for the night.

In the morning and now, the way was finally open and I joined the queues that had appeared from nowhere for the tortuous business of customs and border control. It only took four hours.

Between the penultimate stamped document and the Mongolian border is twenty kilometres of buffer zone. The tarmac was in no great shape and my nerves were starting to show as I slowed down to cope. At the end of the buffer zone stood a tall steel gate with a barbed wire fence running right and left into the far horizon.

The last Russian border guard gave a final flourish and stamp to my documents and swung open the rusty gate.

Like a cheap horror flick, the gate groaned and screeched and the Mongolian steppe stretched before me. Grass, low hills and nothing.

As far as the eye could see. Nothing.

The motorway marked by Google was a three-metre-wide rock and shingle horror story.

DAUNTED

I was daunted.

My Moto Guzzi Stelvio is stalwart but very large. I am fairly small.

When I drop the bike, a fairly frequent occurrence but usually at slow speed, I simply wait for someone to pass and get them to help me upright it. Here there were no people. No motoring organisation recovery. There were no sheep or goats or horse or camels; not a yak or a yurt to be seen. And still another twenty kilometres to the Mongolian customs post.

The lane that leads to my house in England is just minutes from the motorway; riding it always puts me in a good mood because it is narrow and roofed by the branches of massive horse chestnut trees. An English lane: an oasis of calm; we call it semi-rural.

This winter the tarmac had been ripped up. It started with big trucks wearing a few holes when making deliveries to the retirement home at the end of the lane; the remaining residents made it worse as they drive up and down in cars and Zimmer frames.

It is here that I trained for off-road; I stand on the pegs and weave the entire three metres of bad road.

Only one thing for a trained off-road rider to do here in Mongolia; a word with the gods of the road, screw up the courage and onward... the next horizon.

It wasn't good, this introduction to Mongolia. It is not semi urban at all. Struggling through the rock and shingle I thought about riding down the two-metre raised bank of the road and onto the steppe. There were plenty of tracks through the grass; but where were they going? And would I be able to ride back up the shingled bank if I needed to? I thought about my wife and children just about waking up eight time zones behind me – and wondered again why was I here.

And then I rode around a hill and there a thrice blessed concrete road with the customs post standing proud. And yaks, large, shaggy, brown with very long horns feeding in a fenced off field.

The customs post seemed overlarge, concrete chic with shiny polished floors inside. Photos and instructions on the walls, tourist leaflets of attractions to come and I followed a large crowd of five to meet the police and sundry other officials.

Back in London, tripping round embassies gathering visas the Mongolians were the quickest, friendliest and fastest of all. Here, in their own land, they're still smiling and equally quick.

There was some consternation; like the Vegas in Armenia over a year ago, there was no reference on their computers to a Moto Guzzi motorcycle model named as the Stelvio. As yet unlisted and according to them, none had passed through this border. I was the first one in.

I took a moment of pride in possibly being the first solo Motor Guzzi Stelvio rider to enter the Mongolian Nation.

Which was regrettable, for when the purchase of obligatory but worthless vehicle insurance came a few minutes later the price went up for a vehicle unlisted, minimum period being a year.

I eschewed the tourist gift shop. The border with China being just two hundred and fifty kilometres south I doubted much had been made in Mongolia, tourist tat or not.

My relative calm melted quickly; riding east once more into the country the concrete road ended within five hundred metres and the shingle and the steppe returned.

I discovered I could ride down and up the road bank.

A berm built of stones obstructed the road. With no way forward I followed a thin track, down the bank and up again on the flat with the rear wheel spinning in an uncontrolled skid, weight shifted right and accelerate out, to slow down with an instant sheen of fearful sweat coursing down my face. To ask again, to myself in my helmet, why on earth was I here?

A few slow riding hours, one town and several conversations with the gods later I ventured across a smile sitting on a motorcycle at the side of the road. I stopped and in clear mime I asked the smile's owner if I could get a coffee and a night's sleep and petrol at the next town. And where was the next town please?

His smile grew broader and he said, in perfect English, "Follow me." So I did, and off we went across the steppe at a lick of speed with which I was not entirely comfortable. Thirty minutes and a small mountain and large yurt grew out of the horizon. Stopping at the yurt amid a herd of goats he said, "My family." From the yurt, appearing on cue, the father, mother, a brother and two sisters all smiling and greeting "Hello."

Tea was made, greetings done and I signed up for the guided tour.

The yurt was large, circular and about ten metres across, five or more metres high. The frame painted crimson, rare carpets covering walls and the floor.

Five beds next to the walls. Four small singles with a hospital design, shiny, metal and sides that let down and a fifth, for the parents, rather larger, four-postered with nets and brocade.

In the centre, a round table surrounded with fold away chairs, covered with more rich brocade. And a television with a music centre too.

Outside to a low built three room concrete block cottage. Here my new friends live out the worst of the winter in two bedrooms, a kitchen and a bathroom with a hand filled bath.

Mother sits down to cook on a dung powered stove using a very large wok;

I knew not the utensil's local name, but the food looked vaguely familiar.

Outside again and greeting goats, shaggy horses bred for stamina and milk, not speed and twenty first century technology in the shape of a solar powered power plant for batteries and lighting; but not big enough for heating.

Food prepared, we sit down en-famille. The children, all in their early twenties, wore shapeless hoodies and ubiquitous jeans.

Joi, the father, wore a jolly round embroidered hat with his lined and sun-stained face belying his youth, a stripling to me, but aged ancient by the weather, like his wife.

Ji, a.k.a. mother, skin burnt by the sun and wind, wore a blue patterned silk headscarf, a black fleece layer with a gilet on top, synthetic leather fur-lined boots and a surprisingly pretty skirt of black silk painted with pink and cream flowers.

There is poverty here, and life is truly hard, but high spots of joy in colour and traditional things.

Now dinner, and I was right in my earlier assumption, for we are served the feared and famous Mongolian delicacy of plov; boiled rice flavoured with special spherical balls of meat held together with skin, known to the rest of the world as testicles.

It was sustaining if a tad chewy.

On the table too were small golden round rolls of bread, made from, I was assured, strong Russian flour. To drink, fermented mare's milk offered which I declined as being not to my taste and took instead black tea from a delicate hand-painted bowl.

Questions were asked, of my life and my wife in the west. My laptop with pictures shown as I noted my phone, camera and Marmite, proffered to taste, disappearing below the table to be spirited away.

I talked of a home with a garden, but not of the size of the house, and then mentioned two motorcycles and a car, belonging to my wife.

Jio, he with the smile, then said he owned four cows, ten horses, ten camels and a hundred goats. All for travelling, dung and good eating too. Which notion quite rightly, out here on the steppe, put me firmly in my place.

Joi meantime was fiddling at something, with difficulty, with his fingers. From my bag, I offered him my spare pair of spectacles, rimless, varifocal, a respected and reputable brand. Expensive. Probably worth a cow.

He put them on and marvelled that he could suddenly see. And with a smile from ear to ear, golden teeth on show, slipped them into his pocket as a gift.

Outside again in the darkest night I've ever experienced, witnessing such brilliant stars and far off galaxies and knew now what was meant by the term, the Milky Way.

A brother, home for the holidays from studying law at university in next door Kazakhstan, was turfed from his bed which was given over to me; where I slept exhausted, until dawn and the lowing of cattle brought gently out of my sleep.

This morning, a family conference gathered, mother at the helm.

Through Jio's translation some enquiries.

"Had I had a good night's sleep? Had I enjoyed the food?" My affirmations given, another question asked. "Would I then consider making a payment for the traveller's respite given?"

Twenty euros offered and after explanations as to currency and exchange rates considered via the Net, there were smiles, handshakes and Ma and Pa on their Chinese motorcycle off to spend the money in town. With Joi peering through my spectacles, grinning from ear to ear.

An honest assessment of my circumstances followed with just me in charge.

My mind is not always a good place to be in by myself. There are at least three other characters sharing the space but I have learned today, almost, to listen most to the voice that suggests the next right thing.

Twenty or so years ago I was co-owner of a business that lurched too often between affluence and negative cashflow.

I remember, as if it were yesterday, being in my car, a dark navy blue Jaguar saloon, cream leather, walnut fascia and soundproofing so good I could barely hear the gravel spitting from the tyres as I drove at speed on the hard shoulder. Time was stretching, slowing down, dividing into nano seconds. Approaching the bridge I could see in fine detail the water stained concrete, closer still the rust running like blood.

In the grip of fear, financial insecurity and deep depression I had aimed the car, at high speed, at a motorway bridge. My brain had stopped, waiting for my life to end; my heart, slow thudding and metal barrier about to screech when a thought arrived unbidden. "No, not this day. Your death will teach no lessons." With infinite slowness, pressure applied by my right hand and the car was back in the proper lane, indicator flashing, leaving at the next junction.

That I write this today you will realise that the suicide attempt did not work. I mention it as an insight to my mindset in Mongolia.

Back then I had upset my business partner badly; I wanted to move the business onto the web, he wouldn't agree, so I went and asked our biggest competitor for a job in order to exploit the internet. The competitor called my partner to find out more. Enraged, my partner finagled my exit from the company. Part of the finagling was to introduce a new partner; the share balance was no longer equal; he and the new partner had majority shares.

A board meeting was called in my absence. I was voted off the board and fired.

At that time, an affluent period was ending but my expenditures were not reined in accordingly. There was no offer, on being fired, of buying my shares; there was no offer of a couple of month's salary. The assets and cash were transferred, the business closed.

Leaving me haemorrhaging money with no income or immediate prospects. And, as any owner of a small business knows, our personal identity is inseparable from our business. Failure of one is failure of the other. Having a business closed without any recourse is like having a child ripped away from you. And the big question, of shame, of "What will people think?"

My self-centred suicide would have shown the world my pain and taught my ex partners a lesson… or at least that was the thought. But in truth would they care? And if so, so what?

With suicide not working, I had a nervous breakdown instead and went to bed for a couple of months, completely unable to cope.

I recovered, in due course, through the deep love and succour of my family. A very good friend called me daily and gave me a job to regain some self-respect. And at the end of my road a small and beautiful church is host to a twelve-step programme twice a week. One day at a time I returned to life.

I am so very grateful to my family and to my friends who nursed me in my turmoil.

In retrospect, all this seems to be very small beer indeed; but that is only with the advantage of hindsight. I wonder today how I could have allowed myself to be so fearful, to endure so much anguish and most of all to have been so selfish. To want to end my life with no notion of how this would affect my wife, my children. So selfish; but in black

depression the thought is always there...
no-one else can understand the pain.

I have learned that no matter how
difficult situations seem to be, sharing
with a loved one, or a complete stranger,
is the first step to regaining reality. Open
up, speak to another person. And if you
have Faith, then ask for help there too.

I have the understanding; mental
illness, overt stress. Such a dark place.

But I know of others who were not so
fortunate as me. They were alone in the
darkness; they did not recover.

I have learned that I no longer fear my
own death, but feel in advance the sorrow
that will follow for those that I love.

This then, was lurking in the
background as I sat in the Mongolian
sun undergoing self- assessment.

"Be still." I instructed my labouring
heart. "Thus far, and no more."

My ribs were hurting badly as I
considered the following:

Ulaanbaatar, the capital, was seventeen

hundred kilometres hence. Across the barren steppe, on my own.

Was I really set up or prepared for nights alone in a tent, crossing swollen rivers, dropping the bike or puncture repair?

Fuel was hard to come by.

I had only a few Euros, no local currency or Russian roubles either. There seemed to be no ATMs on the steppe.

My dislike of formal planning, or selfish thinking, had brought me down to this. I was here, on my own, and in truth, not having a great deal of fun.

Sensibly I think, I rewrote the mission plan in my head and decided that my goal had been to reach Mongolia, but not to die here all alone.

Decision made I found and retrieved my camera and phone but the Marmite I left behind.

With fervent good wishes, good luck abounding and petrol topped up in the tank, I turned the bike around and headed back towards the west.

HEADING WEST

In pain but in good spirits I rode slowly on the road.

Photographs taken of mountains, the motorcycle posing alone beside a turquoise lake but this time following the sun on down toward the sunset.

Customs and the border easy, no surprise at the length of stay.

In no mans' land a motorcyclist in soft leather jacket on a moto, BMW. Everything brand new. He asks, in Russian, about the road ahead. I know he is asking this because of the fear in his face and the fact he is pointing over my shoulder to the east. I smile and shrug, I am leaving and with the leaving the fear is staying behind. Besides, we're on a Russian tarmac road. His back up crew, in black t-shirts, in a Hummer, look bored. Not a camera between the three minders or the rider to record the epic meet. Starved of another opportunity for potential fame, I smile again and ride on.

Easy now, except at the Russian border post the bike must be bathed in disinfectant before touching true Russian soil. At the bargain price, wheels dipped only, for five Euros cash.

Welcomed in the border town, now respected as a rider of the Mongolian steppe, the yurt offered overnight with no delay and in the morning onto the ripped black Russian tarmac; but after the road of stones there will be no more complaints from me.

To my friends in the Altai oasis, licking my ego and my wounds, a meeting with a mother in law, in a little wooden church, discussing alcoholism and God. And me eternally grateful that I was here to share.

Food, mostly European, a jolly game or two of Hangman and a visit to the nearest town to check on progress of the money due for the sale of the land.

I am heartened by such generosity, deeply grateful for the friendship shown and more than a little emotional when it was time to go.

But I have nine thousand kilometres to cover, and there will be weather, and worse, to overcome.

A RUSSIAN
BIKER PARTY

Three nights further on, I was reasonably lost again. I knew, but again in relative terms, that, as the crow flies I was still more than eight thousand kilometres from home.

I was lost only because I was trying to get out of a city in which I'd just arrived, but had ridden through before, and there wasn't a great deal of signage that I could read or understand.

A traffic policeman flagged me to a stop and I readied myself for the shakedown, but for once it didn't happen. Instead, a thousand-metre convoy of leather clad bikers thundered into view and turned directly right in front of me. When they'd passed I had just one thought – that looks more fun than I'm having here; I'm going where they're going.

With no planning at all I'd arrived at a fine bike rally in Barnaul, a Siberian river port a bit north of the midway point between the borders of Kazakhstan and Mongolia. Following the riders, I found a slew of tents pitched next to the vast Ob river with food stands, rock 'n' roll played shatteringly loud on a large and strobe-lit stage. I was offered as much free booze as I wanted; but with my allergy to alcohol I really had no great desire for any, free or otherwise.

Next to the river's beach, deep holes had been dug and motorcycles inserted, vertically racing to the stars. Their owners, for no other would dare to touch, were seated, eyes to Heaven shouting brmmm brrmm. Each to their own I thought, and sidled past to the bar where a very large, slightly unsteady man accosted me.

"Anglia?" he shouted. Anglia is a region in England so I thought, although from London, I should agree. He said, "You know my brother."

This question and answer session was in one of the green striped canvas covered tents set up as a bar. Having asked the question, he turned away slowly and with a smile, nodding equally slowly and enigmatically to his three friends. His slow movement was primarily designed to keep him upright. Alcohol had already glazed his eyes and his skin had started to mottle a surprising shade of strawberry.

We chatted on in broken English far superior to any attempt I made with Russian and it transpired that I did indeed know his brother; the previous priest on a bike.

Back at the bar I was told it was time for bowling. "You want be the ball?" asked my newest friend. I declined, and happy that I did. Ten pin bowling, Russian biker style, comprises a team of four throwing a man, a.k.a. the ball, the length of a wet tarpaulin to knock over as many of the ten beer bottles as possible.

My oh my, this was fun; with ribs cracked still I was delighted to be an observer rather than a ball.

Monied bikers, and there were many, had rented wooden tents with room enough for four. Outside these stood the Harley's, big Hondas and other large rock 'n' roll machines. This was the territory of the Wolves, a 1% club endorsed by Mr Putin trying to buff his image of power, strength and youth. Mr Putin, photographed, rode a bike with three wheels. Which says it all for now.

Fellow motorcycle travellers were arriving too. From Korea, North and Western Europe.

Some had visited before – a Norwegian, string bean tall and older than me had ridden here for the third time and was feted by the crowd.

I noted the travellers, impecunious, lived, like me, in a tent.

Beautifully customised Urals, Dniepers in profusion, with and without sidecars.

From further west, a clutch of Jawas but mainly imports from China and Japan. Of Moto Guzzi, only one.

I was parked next to a first edition Vmax; and when asked for a traveller's tale I was inspired to tell of 2006, an Iron Butt race to Faro, Portugal on my own Vmax. Of stair-rod rain and on the Spanish plateau, heat enough to melt the paint. I had nitrous, in a bottle fully charged but when running out of petrol a catheter, stolen from my mother in law, was deployed, quite often, to fill the too small tank.

I'd been fed for free by an adoptive bunch of ex-Spetsnaz warriors and their women who'd cooked up an enormous and continuously replenished cauldron of borscht, served with hard brown bread. The women were brave, and swam in the nude with others in the Ob.

I did not.

KARLAG

A new road, border and a modern hotel.

But first some Russian traffic cops on the side of the road with a video gun.

They flag me down and I stop the bike. Helmet and gloves removed, crossed the road and after handshakes all round, there is a companionable silence as we watch the video together.

One hundred and ten, should have been ninety.

I smile. They smile.

"Britanski?"

"Da."

"Manchester United?"

"Da."

"Nice bike, go."

And I'm gone to the south west with a good wind at my back for five hundred kilometres more until I see a low concrete block with a green flag in which I negotiate insurance cover for the country I'm about to enter.

To border police and customs, everything easy. Into the Kazak section and I copy details from the form submitted in Russia and it's stamped and I'm riding ahead.

Low sun in my eyes and into the city of Semey to overnight in the unremarkable modern hotel.

I've been invited to stay on a couch in Karaganda, twelve hours in the saddle from here. The days are still long and I'm told the roads are moderate to good.

Which they are, with something not fully expected. The wind, my first taste of the Buran, is roaring but the sky remains blue and I'm happy. Except I ride for four hours at a constant lean angle; more like sailing than riding.

This then, is the true steppe. Semi-arid, sometimes semi-desert and nothing, almost nothing from horizon to horizon for hours and hours and hours punctuated by petrol stations and the tarmac road melting in the sun.

To give you a better idea of nothing; Kazakhstan is the ninth largest country on Earth, with a population less than that of Los Angeles.

The almost nothing is constituted of the occasional lonely man trudging to who knows where.

I did meeet a fellow motorcyclist. We are both riding toward each other on a single lane, lonely track with the steppe on either side and nothing else to see. We approach, slow down, stop and both dismount. He is Russian with some English and has a sheepskin over his seat. I am English with no Russian.

This is a transcript of the conversation.

"Hi, benzene?"

Pointing behind him he raises ten fingers, six times.

"Allo, benzene?"

I point behind me, raising ten fingers ten times.

We both smile. A hug. We're back on our bikes and rolling away. In truth, what more was there to say?

And the other almost nothings are far off yurts, and riders slowly following herds of horses through the sea of golden grass. Always though, and consistently, a friendly wave from these most isolated men.

Finally, the city, Karaganda, which was to shock to me to the core.

As I've described already there is a similarity to the cities of the former USSR; in the suburbs everywhere poured concrete apartment blocks all built under Mr Khrushchev's rule.

Although disliked by some today, back then they had new kitchens and bathrooms, and best of all, behind locked doors.

So, on High Street, Karaganda. Turn right in the gloaming at this café then left on the pavement and outside this very large steel door.

To phone and find Katrina who taps down the steps and opens the door and pins me to the wall with dazzling smile.

She looks sixteen but claims two more added years. I think she may have lied about her age on her Couchsurfing profile and I'm not entirely comfortable.

But needs must and its five floors, no lift and as I'm here for two or three days it's a complete luggage lift and shift. Katrina, thank God, is young fit and used to running the stairs. She's been up and down twice, with cases, before I've made it once.

And then she cooks, but its late, I'm really very tired so it's the couch and the arms of Morpheus for me.

In the morning, I discover that her father, who I'm about to meet, bought the apartment for her while she studies for her degree. She shares it with a cousin, the latter currently in the country with her own family for the holidays.

The interrogation, for the protection of the daughter, is in two parts. First Katrina's mother on the boardwalk of a smart café.

The family is from Russian stock; mother, once a teenage bride and still in her thirties, is slim, beautiful, cornsilk hair and coiffed, perfect nails with discreet gold on her throat and at the wrist and wears a very short skirt. And very high heels.

She has some English. We talk of family and flirt in a low-key way. She's amusing and amused and would prefer to live in Europe. We get on very well and I'm declared to be safe.

Katrina's father is different kettle of fish, making his living as a Roof.

In Kazakhstan too, in these dangerous days, men of middle rank power and influence need protection from rapacious gangsters seeking to take-over businesses in ways that are far from legal.

Those in need of protection hire a Roof. The Roof puts his hands in a steeple over their heads and protects them. With violence meted out to those who would show too much business interest.

So I am now being grilled by a violent gangster about my relationship with his teenage daughter. He's large, both tall and wide; blonde hair going to grey, wide face, snub nose and by the look of him, very strong. Blue jeans, dark shirt stretched over muscle, hard hands, a broken nail and thick gold at his neck.

Fortunately, I pass his test too. It is my age I think and physical form. I am like a small stick having lost three kilos somewhere since I left home.

We talk of east and west and of his desire, unlike his wife, to go nowhere.

"I have everything I want in my country," he said, "I can ride in the desert in the morning then shoot wild pigs and wolves and bear in the mountains in the forest in the afternoon."

Unlike his wife who'd rather be in Bond Street's shops or me, who'd prefer to talk about anything other than guns.

Interrogation over, unnecessary any water boarding, and Katrina decides we will go to see a famous local band. In rehearsal.

The band's name is forgotten to me; metal rock of some kind and she's a groupie already known to them. I understand this visit is actually a demonstration for me; to show she's known by the regional and famous youth.

It's not hard to chat to persons younger than my daughters; I understand their curiosity, nervousness covered by bravura, seeking affirmation. And I am fascinated by an education process, nationalism, youthful cynicism, collective shame and hard edged economics seen through the eyes of the young.

In Kazakhstan corruption is mainly nepotic i.e. from nepotism, not sex with a body past its sell-by date. The previous generations of ruling ethnic Russians are being deposed and Kazakhs, their brothers, sisters and cousins thrice removed are taking over all the jobs.

The bigger corruption, or grand theft, is with the President.

Kazakhstan is fabulously wealthy; oil and gas just seep from the ground. Here in Karaganda there's coal being mined and steel mills rolling through the night.

Young people, under twenty-five, think their President for life is a most wonderful man. The older population watch the billions of dollars sliding to his trouser pocket and may question, but say nothing.

I have decided it bothers me not. There is worse to consider here.

We're off on the bike in the morning to the village of Dolinka; home of Karlag, or more correctly, the Karaganda Corrective Labour Camp of which I had not previous knowledge.

"I cried." said Katrina "When we visited here with my school."

We parked outside a smart white and grey styled, as Russians call it, second Empire building. Built on two floors with a basement, decorated with Doric columns and an immense Red Star, previously an administrative centre, now housing a museum.

And walked into a sanitised depiction of hell, here on earth.

I read the words, written by an inmate.

"Let my hand against its will convey the horror, convey the unimaginable and indescribable nature of what is hidden behind the words 'prison' and 'camp'.

Stalin stares, his face two metres tall. Blood red background, watchtowers in the graphic.

I pass, with increasing horror, sadness and shared shame from room to room. Harrowing photographs of families and individuals arriving on trains and by cart. Children wrenched from parents, tears and outstretched fingers. Women, pregnant, hauled off to separate camps. Men with drawn faces, hungry, showing their bones. And pictures of those in uniform, smart, men and women, smiling.

Here are original cattle trucks for the movement of prisoners, solitary confinement cells, blood and nail marks on the wall, waxworks of men under torture.

This is a museum mind; thankfully we cannot hear the cries of torture, cracking of whips or smell the day to day smells.

I need to share some numbers.

The Karlag was not just one but a connected group of forced labour camps throughout this area of Kazakhstan. All run from this small building.

Consider the size of the camp.

Two hundred kilometres east to west; three hundred kilometres north to south. That's twice the size of Belgium. Almost two million hectares of agriculture and farms slave-laboured for food for the proud young Republic when Stalin's Soviet policies caused famine across the land.

Karlag. A different kind of collective effort.

The camp was started in 1930. It was reportedly closed, when, for those who still remember, the launches of BMW R27, Ducati's Bronco, the Norton Navigator and Royal Enfield's Interceptor. For those who don't, Ford Cortinas were becoming the most popular car.

Reportedly closed means the camps were officially reorganised and run by 'Places of Detention Administration'.

I'd already ridden past, that day, a Place of Detention; a vast white concrete prison complex, still in existence and business continued.

In the socialist paradise, Stalin's paranoia required large numbers of people to be removed from society to the Gulag's secret custody. In all, eighteen million souls.

I ask myself, how can any nation lock up this many political protesters? Then note the largely muted opposition in Russia still today.

Of these eighteen million, a million or more human beings passed through the Karlag; but this only an estimated number, as the records remain secret and sealed.

First the prisoners built a railway, then grew food exported by the railroad to keep the elite of Moscow and Western Russia from fomenting more revolution.

As an aside, in the Thirties, forty percent of the Kazakh population died from starvation or fled. Kazakhs became the minority in their own country.

Eventually with targets, goals and punishments the camps became a major contribution to the Soviet economy.

And why not? For Soviet economists, apart from human degradation, the labour cost was free.

The camp was not just agriculture. Mining and metallurgical industries established then are still important today; there were scientists too, jailed for who knows what, engaged in ground-breaking research.

The camp was filled first, with racist bias, by thirty thousand Chechen Muslims, moved en-masse from the east.

Then, in alphabetical order:

Belarusians

Chechens

Estonians

Finns

French

Georgians

Germans

Hungarians

Ingush

Italians

Japanese

Jews

Kazakhs

Kyrgyz

Latvians

Lithuanians

Poles

Romanians

Russians

Ukrainians.

And Aleksandr Solzhenitsyn, writing 'One Day in the Life of Ivan Denisovich'. Although Aleksander was later sent to a camp further north.

In all, there are some one hundred and thirty nationalities living in Kazakhstan today, most originally coming from the families of the previously enslaved.

It is informative, but bleak, this museum.

I am left with a feeling of ineffable sorrow, especially knowing this inhumanity still continues all round the world.

Katrina, in sorrow and shame for her forbears and to change and uplift the mood announces a party.

With a special theme.

Night of the Bong

On our return and in the kitchen young men, some from the band of the previous night, are mixing a concoction of mainly tobacco and other ingredients as yet unrecognised by me.

In the days of my drinking and drugging we mixed up coloured alcohol in cocktails, and could be found inhaling hand rolled smokes; but nothing, nowhere near, as complex as this.

I knew this equipment; referred to, by me, as a Hookah available freely for hippies and hipsters at home or in cafes of the ethnic kind.

But today, for the less literate and perhaps for the purpose of branding, it is evidently called a Bong.

There is a mash of some sort, reddish orange in colour, prepared and ready.

The Bong, a slim forty centimetres of elegant blown glass has a tall cylinder with a flexible tube and mouthpiece mounted at the top and on the bottom, a large round water filled ball as the base. The stem, a hollow tube with a receptacle hold the lit and glowing mash connected to the bottom, through the water in said ball.

Smoke is filtered by water and sucked out into the participant's lungs and brain.

In my day, a cigarette holder was a close as I got to this. Or a rolled-up banknote.

With neither drugs or drink in my life anymore I watch without comment as the party worked the pipe.

My contribution, taken not given, was, it was decided, that each person who sucked on the bong, with the exception of Katrina, must wear, during the act of suction, the chrome coated steel helmet of German design acquired as a gift from an insistent ex Spetnatz warrior two days before.

Of the helmet, after this date, I saw no more. Perhaps it is now a folkloric tradition for Bong parties throughout Kazakhstan.

However, I was not comfortable with these circumstances; vegetable matter taken in smoke and young people and me at least twice and a half their age. I was happy when the party was shifted to booze in the bars on the street.

Maintenance

Without advanced electronics getting in the way, most motorcycle mechanicals can be done by anyone competent.

However, and hitherto, I'm not.

The insides of engines are a mystery and I've liked to have kept it that way. But I do understand about regular maintenance and with the battering the bike's taken to date I thought I should have it reviewed.

The manual says the valve gaps should be monitored, every eight thousand kilometres. Now I'm not truly sure what that means; but I'd downloaded the manual to my laptop and my phone so that I could show someone what they had to do.

Up to a small lockup, gleaming inside and open for business as a mechanic, with motorcycles on the floor and spanners hung neatly on the walls. The mechanic comes highly recommended by Katrina's rock band friends.

My laptop is open showing the maintenance guide, pictures of valves and other things. My man downloads the file to a stick, uploads to his own computer, checks he can read it and says with a smile "Come back in a couple of hours."

He's not just a mechanic. He works without showing a taxable income and he's the President of the local moto gang. So I cannot write his name. I'll call him Vlad. And then I asked where to buy tyres; front and rear both looking a bit worse for wear.

Katrina, who came for the ride, on the phone to her father for help.

He arrives and we're off to the moto mart, a collection of previously industrial buildings now set up as stalls with sprockets, gear boxes, wheels and all sorts of oil.

After an hour of asking, it's evident that none of the tyres on offer would fit the Italian, out here in Kazakhstan.

So onward we seamlessly move to the next challenge; petrol, a portable can.

We find a five-litre plastic container, empty and cleaned out of oil. And a bright orange nylon strap to fix it to the bike.

Thus prepared and back to the lockup I collect the valve readied motorcycle, now cleaned into the bargain too.

Small money changed hands, Katrina pretty as she perched on the pillion and we're off back to the town.

Dinner with her friends in a café but it's an early night for me.

In the morning, goodbye and huge hugs from this small and vibrant person. I'll miss her, it's been fun.

BUILDING BLOCKS

I could have ridden the steppe directly east toward Russia but I'd been warned of long lonely roads, no villages and lack of working petrol stations.

So it was north for a few hundred kilometres to the nation's brand new capital, Astana.

It hasn't been the capital city for long; the President for Life decided new was the new order. And the centre of the country was best. So he built Astana, sucking the money and the power from someone else's powerbase in Almaty, in the south.

When in other people's countries, I try to find and speak of similarities; I'm here to learn, sharing my version of the differences only when I'm asked. I don't always succeed but to do otherwise, I believe, might be considered bragging or disparaging and worse still, a crashing bore.

But this new bright and shiny capital is, well, not really to my taste.

There are new buildings in profusion

designed by famous men. Japanese, the English and others.

Convince me please that trees with artificial pink blossoms made from glass beads are a step forward in architecture.

In my landscaping career, for special effect we'd lay down flagstones that naturally glittered and match them to a fence-line painted with glitter, to be discovered sparkling in the headlights in the night.

But nothing prepared me for the beads or the artificial beach.

For all the world, the architecture looked like pre-school building blocks tumbled from a giant child's hands, not plastic, but still multi-coloured now fashioned from steel and glass.

And the location. There is nothing, then the city and then nothing again. In all directions, flat. Only the steppe.

Uncomfortable, I stayed in a small hotel When I was lost in the morning, a kindly man in a car on the school run with his son diverted from his journey and led me to the city limits, and pointed me north.

The Cafe
in Nowhere

I'm heading north partly because I've been invited by a man and his family to visit with them in Kostanay, in the west near the Russian border. But to reach them, because of the roads, I must go north three hundred kilometres to Kokshetau then turn left and ride four hundred more.

There's nothing of particular interest as I ride. Just long empty roads, nondescript villages, the occasional petrol station, horsemen with their herds, cattle and few camels. Although camels are usually much further south.

Then a storm whipped up from nowhere; raining truly, madly, deeply.

I stopped at the extension, or so it seemed, to a very small refinery of oil or maybe something agricultural. In truth, I was too tired to find out more as I happened on the mass of storage tanks and pipes surrounded on all sides by a bleak reinforced concrete three-metre-high walls. It was the attendant café and shelter that got my interest most.

It was all very Kazakh – nothing, storm, nothing, storm, refinery with café...

I stopped, drenched, hoping the storm, would pass but it hasn't; it's seven 'o' clock and I really don't want to ride further into nothing.

I've eaten, something with rice and omnipresent cucumber on the side, the place is empty and the staff, two women, dark haired, dark eyed and now the subject of a nice photograph in my camera., are trying to close.

I do my second-best mime – that of where can I sleep? Understood and out of the café and next door into a small single room with a hand basin, rusting and water running, affixed to the wall. There's a bed of sorts, with a grubby brown cover and really not much more.

It's a couple of thousand tenge for the night. I'm not about to argue especially as I calculate its less than five British pounds. They give me a key. In the café I buy some chocolate, a litre of water and pay for the room. Cash only, cards not accepted here.

I move the bike under a cover, blocking the café entrance and manage to secure the gate behind it. Why I should be suddenly worried by thieves four hundred kilometres from anywhere is beyond me. Perhaps I feel like some exercise, more likely because there's nothing to do.

Undo my luggage, gas stove, pot, steel cup and very good coffee to be made in my Aero-press pression. It is a simple device, a tube in three parts. Filter at the bottom, add coffee, pour water and press. Presto. Delicious Lavazza, carried thus far with a spoonful of sugar found in my pack.

Now with light failing I'm back in my room and discover there's no power for the light. The night passes, darkly, with scratching and other assorted small noises.

In the morning cockroaches slip from their bedroom as I upturn my boots. And a small lizard scurries out to the sunlight when I open the door.

It's early; but I see no reason to lay longer in a bed with no springs. A cat's lick for a wash, as my mother used to say, coffee made and drunk and I'm pushing the bike backwards, but it's stuck. It has no reverse gear; there's no room at the side for pushing or pulling. I climb over a wall to the carpark where a truck has pulled up in the night and I bang on the door for assistance. More mime, and the driver gets out. Me on the bike, him shoving and I'm clear. A million thanks, hands shaken and smiles and I'm away in the sunshine, more or less at the break of the day.

I passed my host's city, Kostanay, late in the day and sent a text to say I couldn't make it.

I didn't mind the thousand-kilometre loop that had been added to my journey but I was weary, hollowed out, still experiencing sharp shafts of pain and wouldn't have been good company.

I wanted nothing more than a night in a hotel, with clean sheets and a shower.

So I kept riding until I found one. Ate something with more cucumbers on the side, cleaned up, slept well.

WHO THE HELL ARE YOU?

I rode away, refreshed, in the morning.

Four hundred kilometres forward since I last turned south, over this small hill, and I see a man on a bicycle. Unusual I thought and give him a wave as I pass, the first human I'd seen for more than three hours. I ride on, no time to stop for I'm hungry for more petrol, even the spare container is empty so it needs to be soon.

At the side of the road a small white building with wooden decorations painted blue. There's a parking space in the gravel out front, and sun protecting awning stretched out at the side. A man is sitting in the shade.

Bike now running on fumes, I pull over to inquire. "No petrol." said the man in the shade, "We're a café, want eggs?"

He called to his wife who worked out back, perspiring and cooking in an extension the size of a toilet.

I accepted the eggs. Fried, underdone and had some ham too, turning down the proffered cucumbers of which I have had too many.

With my back to the road I do not see the lone cyclist until he was upon us. Out of the saddle he stood, exceptionally tall in black shorts and cyclists blue top emblazoned with the words Pedal for Parkinson's in contrasting white. He was sun bleached European, sleek muscles shining from exertion, hair slightly receding, side burned, suntanned and smiling.

Well met, I thought, but here, almost as far as you could get from anywhere in the steppe, he ups and comes forward, hand outstretched in greeting and said, "Hello, I'm Paul. Are you Derek Mansfield?"

How now, what's this? I'm stunned. Shocked silence. I look around in case there's a camera crew hiding, filming a version of 'This is your life.' Have my creditors reached out to find me?

He orders some tea and sits down, with a smile, to explain.

Paul is on an epic journey cycling home from Xiamen, a city over the straits opposite Hong Kong where he taught English, to a small town south of London in the countryside of Sussex.

He rides to support a charity that supports, in turn, people with Parkinson's, a loathsome illness that his father has contracted.

We are both, he explained, couch-surfing through Kazakhstan and due to stay with the same people in a few days. The people ahead had said look out for Derek, and here and now, in this wilderness together, we drank tea.

Extraordinary meeting with an extraordinary man; made of very tough stuff. Sleeping with wolves, cycling through storms in the mountains; how I looked forward to hearing much more.

But I could not tarry at this moment; we rode at different speeds and I had petrol to find. "No worry," said the café owner, "benzene in five."

He meant fifty.

At the side of the road, stopped, not much further forward. And I'm going no further at all without refined liquid energy.

I'm watching a man, chopping up fallen branches to put into his car.

Off with the helmet and gloves, crossing the hot road with a spring in my step trying to look friendly, not desperate.

Some mime to explain the predicament. No petrol, moto won't go. He nods understanding and he's on the phone to a friend with a smile then a frown. Three times he does this and then shakes his head…. Obviously no-one around to ferry petrol for a biker stuck here.

Back to the bike, plastic oil can and catheter tube. With his permission, I'm sucking liquid into the can. Money exchanged, joyous hugs and I'm pouring the precious petrol into my tank; on the bike and onwards.

But the three litres doesn't go far even at optimum slow speed, which is why I'm cruising this hamlet, eyes like gimlets, looking for more. A Ural I see with a sidecar in the garden next to a very old silvered, timbered, worn out cottage.

I park, approach and knock on the door at the back. A man of middle age, but looking older, wearing three days of beard opens the door with caution. He is wearing baggy black trousers, vest and shirt to match and incongruous carpet slippers. I have brought with me the plastic petrol can and shake it. "Pazhalsta, mozhna?" "Please may I?", I think I've just said.

Understanding dawns, I'm ushered in. He shouts toward another room. A young woman, his daughter perhaps, arrives. The kettle now on, she leaves, for we are to take tea. The daughter returns, this time with a little lipstick on display which he noticed, looks at me and shakes his head with a wry smile. I think there is not much company out here in this spot. But for her in one package, is a travelling stranger from a fabled land faraway.

I'm charmed by the effort and we speak all three in broken Russian, broken English, good mime and explanatory sketches on paper. And eat some home-made cake.

Next is a tour of their home, three more rooms to see. Two bedrooms and in a third larger space with dark and heavy Soviet table, chairs, velour couch and a book case full of glass and china a dominating Japanese TV. We stand while he flicks through fifty channels. World over, we all agree, the rubbish on daytime TV…

Some petrol now; he's explained there's a town just ten somethings further on.

They are so kind these people. They have so little, and they are happy to give so much away.

No money is needed, hands firmly shaken, regret in the eyes of and smile from the girl, leg over the saddle and in minutes, it's true, here's a town.

With fresh petrol and water, Snickers bars and Coca Cola for the journey forward.

Two hundred more kilometres have spun under the wheels. The sun's been conquered by dark clouds and with the wind freshening fast I've decided it's enough for today. There's a camp site advertised near here but I can't find it and the wind is coming on strong so I find another small hotel in a town called Karabutak, next to a railway line where I'm happy to stay the night.

The family who own it are most friendly; we sit at a table chatting. The grandfather from the east near the Pacific Ocean, his daughter looking western, her husband born also in the east.

Their teenage son tries hard to translate and we come, in the end, to an understanding, which is this. Friendship must always be valued; anywhere you live.

The Buran

I'm laying in the road, choking on dust, whiling away the nanoseconds as the Kamaz truck comes to halt a metre from my head.

A man appears from out of the dust. He saw me go down in his mirror as he overtook and with guilt has doubled back to help. The Kamaz driver is out of the cab and onto the road. He's stopped more traffic piling past with his truck at an angle and now, with the other driver, helps to pull the bike off me and upright, onto its side stand.

The road bed has been dug out to the depth of a metre below the surrounding steppe and back filled with sand and soft crushed rock. The road itself is perhaps six metres wide at best. No room for the kind of mistake that I find myself in.

I'm still winded badly, ribs are felt grinding, can't breathe so they pull me up too but with the newest pain preventing me from putting any weight on my foot.

I look around, see a pannier, the top box and petrol carrier strewn on the road. Adrenalin still coursing, I'm trying to hop; both men make me sit down and be still whilst they recover the luggage and put it on the truck.

One, the man who took me out on the road with his big SUV says in English, "Are you ok?"

I cannot speak to him of niceties and polite driving manners so I gave off a restrained grunt. Not really his fault, though his driving style was not of the best. It was my fault using the front brake in loose sand; I'd done this to myself.

"There is a motel," he advises, first in Russian and then in halting English, "twenty kilometres ahead. Can you ride that far?"

There's no choice. The last town is a hundred kilometres back.

There's no emergency AA call out here, no pick up for the bike. Nor an ambulance on wheels or helicoptered in to soothe me with blankets, ice bags, maybe cups of tea. So it's onward, and slowly, with constant prayers running through my head.

They help me mount the bike. The damaged foot and ankle is on the right and tightening in my boot. I can still operate the gears on the left.

At last, the motel, optimistically painted but now dust scoured dirty pink with a car park full of trucks fifty metres back from the road. I've got my luggage round me, now duct taped and secure and it's all lashed on with duct tape and nothing broken, at least on the bike, just squashed and angled wrongly.

The motel's manager is friendly and concerned and thinks I should stay here the night. The storm's still bad, the sun is lower in the sky.

"No," I said, "thank you, but I'm English, busy, I simply must get on."

Which I did for fifty metres and thence in sand lost the steering again and lay once more on the floor.

The manager looks down at me and sais, "I think you must stay.". As some hefty truckers pick up the bike and wheel it off and I can only agree, thence hobbling and hurting to the seventies plastic reception to check in.

Up to my room. My ankle is badly swollen, much as I expected. I've wrapped it tight with a wet towel which I also wet down frequently to keep the evaporation going. And after an hour, from my medical kit a bandage also wrapped, overlapped and tight. And swallowing painkilling pills in hope.

There's no hospital, doctor or paramedic anywhere close; time to grin and bear it.

There have been other winds on other days. The worst when I was a surface sailor on Her Majesty's Ship Dido, a new, and at that time, modern frigate deep at sea in the Indian Ocean. A hurricane we sailed through, the waves higher than the mast, two thousand four hundred tons swooping up the crest of a wave and crashing down into the trough. But no fear then, even when the ship lurched badly and I was thrown into a steel bulkhead that smashed my nose and removed two teeth. No fear then when I was young and immortal, and trained for battle at sea.

In the morning after a night with little sleep the swelling has reduced and turned a fetching shade of purple, highlighted with mauve. But hobbling still pains me so I must hop downstairs to breakfast.

The voices in my head are all still shouting at once.

"Fool."

"Stay here."

"Ride on."

"Fool."

The trouble is this. In Kazakhstan, they've had a problem with bad roads for a very long time, but no-one cared for a long time either because there were few cars in the cities and none at all in the country. As in Russia, if you were going long distance you went by train or air.

But since Perestroika they'd got their country back, ramped up oil and gas production and people found the money to buy cars, go out and explore. To find that the roads were dreadful and everyone complained.

Russia and Kazakhstan are both enormous; but even with all the resources at their disposal they'll never finish repairs. The extremes of climate alone will see to that.

In Kazakhstan, the road repair programme is extreme too. A hundred kilometres of road are closed. Parallel, usually within sight of the tarmac, a temporary road bed is bulldozed then backfilled with sand and shingle and left for the vehicles to flatten.

You ride the temporary road, back to tarmac long enough for your nerves to calm and then plunge down another sandbank with the fear rising and car drivers passing annoyed with your plight and slow progress.

It isn't good.

The surface constantly changes from solid to shingle to sand; intense concentration needed all the time. Especially on two wheels with few petrol stations open.

"Yeah but…" "Yeah but…" "Yeah but…" "Yeah but…" This in my head. And no way around it. This journey and road was my choice to make.

And the choice now is onward. Everything buttoned up, no charge, I'm delighted to say, for a traveller in distress.

Petrol in the tank and the plastic can brimming too. To the edge of the road leaning left to favour my leg. Nothing here but sand and fear and a long sincere prayer for help.

There is a skill for sand riding. Stand up, lean back, let the front wheel go where it wants and steer with your knees on the tank, leaning left or right. Simple and fun if you've done the off-roading course. But I haven't, except on my lane at home that sported no sand at all. So it's slow ahead, gently.

I didn't count the kilometres switching from sand to tarmac and back to the horror. But it was seven hours of pain with the spare fuel can empty too before the road of repairs was over.

In Uralsk

I was invited to a Gaelic Rock Concert to be treated like a minor celeb.

My host was a rock concert promoter and runs the Uralsk English Speaking Club. For a non-Kazakh speaking Anglo that was quite useful too.

I was to have stayed with the rock promoter, but she's got the headline singer in her apartment; he's younger, fit, good looking with lustrous long black hair. So I'm assigned to the house of a surgeon.

My surgeon is an ethnic Russian, playing guitar and balalaika between cutting people up all day. A look at my foot, and ribs. "All cracked, no treatment," she explains, "nothing to be done." Except here's some painkilling pills and some anaesthetic gel.

It has to be said she's not a great cook, hates doing things on the chopping board and prefers to swig booze from the bottle before breaking out in song. She's also blonde and wears bright lipstick and cares little for neighbours and convention. In short, a very good woman.

In most of the former Soviet Union professionals working for the state earn very little. Teachers make their money selling parents extra books, doctors take bribes for appointments and road menders, well they have two jobs with most money coming from private enterprise, not the income from the State.

Back before Perestroika people were allocated housing by need, not social class. So everyone lived cheek by jowl and only in private did they speak of their superior minds. When the USSR crumbled, the housing was given to the incumbents. And the State factories gave land, in lieu of wages, to employees they couldn't pay. The people went back to the land, built dachas and grew beets and potatoes to survive.

Next day with company; the aforesaid assembly of Uralsk English Speaking Club, to the river to bathe. There are dogs and goats on the footpath to the river; I'm trying to show no fear. Good that the women who are leading me forward are at the front and do not see my nervous skips. That turned into hobbles and pain across my face.

It's strange, I find, that these immense rivers have beaches, and sandy ones at that. I guess, but will not research, that this land was once covered by ocean. Or maybe it's just crushed crumbs of rock from the source up yonder in the mountains. Who knows. Here is a large bronze bust of a famous unknown Soviet writer, and river beach made of sand. On which beach I sit and watch others disporting; I'm retired on medical grounds. People swim, laugh and cavort. I sit and think and wonder that I made it here at all.

Next, we're off to the surgeon's dacha. Veg to be selected and eaten, flowers picked for the hair. They are such fun these English speakers, I'm enamoured of each one. Two are Kazakh, Central Asian. One, the group photographer, big and jolly has solid German genes, another, my surgeon, a Russian and fifth, the rock promoter, has bloodlines indeterminant, a mix of all kinds. The dacha, unvisited for weeks, had grown and spread in profusion, colour splashed with nature's brush. Lilies for the gloss black hair of the Khazaks, something in blue for the blondes.

The dark-haired rock promoter was cooler. She smoked enhanced smile tobacco instead.

We dug deeper for vegetables to find most already eaten by animals that scurry. Grapes in bunches, hung yellow and heavy; on the ground the last of bright ripe melons turning into gold. The door of dacha is opened; we step in and back in time. An old four ringed cooker, its oven still painted original cream and green.

Wooden shelves on white walls in varied states of collapse but still carrying tins and jars of jam and pickled tomatoes, red, yellow and brown. But not, because I'm not brave enough, to be tasted by me.

The surgeon, seems also to be a painter of quality too. Cupboards and doors decorated with still life images frame ageing brass containers and a large copper and black iron weighing machine of the kind remembered from my youth. Light, from the window, delicately coloured and dusty, highlights metal jugs and cups on a hand painted table. None of this retro or repurposed vintage; just beautiful and simple, from fifty years ago.

The group has dissolved and gone to shower and preen. It's the night of the Gaelic Rock concert; a famous band from Moscow, guitars and ukuleles, accordions and drums. Me to a hotel to meet them, and fine guys they turn out to be. Perhaps because they're fascinated by the man on a motorcycle from Mongolia, who is charmed by their attention. And who is now in the bar being interviewed for a national news magazine about travel, but mostly wanting to know how I can run a business remotely, over there, in Ukraine.

My fifteen minutes of fame are over, and we're in a fleet of cars, carried to the venue, hyped up and ready to rock. I can't say I've ever been a fan of the Ceilidh but these Russian's aren't half bad and I'm sitting next to the Kazakh girls, in the intermissions, learning of their lives. It is, it appears, the same the whole world over.

Tall and willowy Elena with deep and soulful eyes, a teacher, wistful and exquisitely polite has a young son. But also, a husband who took women at his pleasure and beat her in another city and now she's on the run. She has a Roof though. Her Roof's real and special name is Lissat (which means Pleasure) Satinova; she's the pocket-sized Asian beauty sitting on my left. Stunning black eyes, cheek bones sharp with full red lips she's having an affair going nowhere with a boring married colleague whose wife no longer cares. The devil-take-it surgeon is now fifty and back to being single, black roots in her bottle blonde hair, molars gone and one incisor yellow, gleaming, made from gold.

Yet all of them seem happy, up and dancing to the band. And later at the surgeon's apartment, more drinks and pickled food; sausages and cheese, gales of laughter as the Balalaiki is strummed and all sing along and the doorbell rings and here stands Paul who has cycled non-stop and caught me up on the night before I leave.

He's through the door with bicycle too and the party gets rowdier until we tire, the girls go home, I'm sleeping on a trestle and Paul, too tall, gets the choice of the floor.

In the morning hugs with this brave man, not knowing then that I would meet him on the road in the future. Twice. I'd like to come back to meet these great people too. More hugs, kisses and tears in the eyes of the rock promoter because we haven't talked enough, and I'm riding forward on good roads in the city, onward to be banned from the country because I don't believe in bribes.

Into the countryside and the roads deteriorate quickly. More bulldozed repairs with sand and shingle but the prayers work and in three hours I'm up to the border, shaken, shaking and glad to be going back to Russia, just for a break.

The border police check my papers, all seems fine but then find the teeniest problem. I didn't register my presence with the police when first I entered the country. I knew about this in Russia and followed all the rules.

You stay in a good hotel, your passport is held overnight and taken to a police department where a document is prepared and stamped which states that you're officially here, or there. I didn't know this same rule was used here in Kazakhstan.

I'd stayed in two hotels who had the sophistication, but to do it, I didn't. Now I cannot leave the country until I have this document.

A senior officer is summoned, the situation explained and I walk with him and a guard, armed, to his office. I am shown a chair, sit down and he fires up his computer.

My passport, visa and entry point are validated and established, why do I not have a registration document? I didn't know, I say. Ignorance is no defence it seems, under their laws too. The solutions are laid out for my inspection.

I can ride back seventy kilometres on a decrepit road to a decrepit town, find a policeman and get the registration documentation. Or I can pay a medium size undocumented fine. I'm not sure what I'm hearing. But I know enough to know that I will not, under any circumstance, ride that terrible road again.

It seems then, we must escalate the information flow officially and I must now have an interpreter who will explain, so that I will completely and in detail understand the repercussions if I do not pay the fine.

The interpreter is summoned. From the town back down the road to which I will not go. Two hours crawl past. I am treated well, given tea. The interpreter, a pretty, dark haired, friendly bouncy woman wearing an ethnic blouse and smart short skirt with stockings and black high heels and came here in her car. To underline she is professional and official.

The solutions are repeated, but have changed in that payment of the medium sized fine is now no longer required.

Or spoken of.

I can still ride back and find a policeman who is willing and obliged to provide me with a registration document. If not, I can have my passport stamped to leave but not return for a minimum of four years. Unless, to obviate the ban, I pay a large fine of three hundred euros electronically by bank draft within the next thirty days. From anywhere on earth. No contest; as much as I adore the denizens of the English Speaking Club I've already said goodbye.

Stamp please.

And it's done and we're friendly and I'm taken up to the head of queue and sent onward, not to return.

Return to Russia

It seems that entry into Russia from the east is simpler than coming from the west.

Or perhaps, because I was careful to keep all the previous paperwork, I make fewer mistakes.

I'm waved to the front of the medium sized queue, documents handed over and perused. It's not until I've cleared all the hurdles and I'm set on the road that I realise half of my motorcycle ownership document has become detached and disappeared, being torn at the fold through constant use.

One of those moments. Do I return and ask them to scour their offices and find my piece of paper? And how do I ask them to do that? Or do I ride on and hope to blag my way through?

Blag wins. In the future, I'll bring two.

Sun in my face and forward to meet a woman who phoned my office in Kyiv and said, "Would love to have him stay." With questions in the voice of the person who relayed the request to me.

I've spent too much time at the border, it's now late afternoon and a five-hour ride without getting lost and stopping for petrol. So more likely to be seven and the sun is levelling down.

The road is black tar, off-times rocky, and the repair crews are out but no diversions of the Kazakhstani kind. Here are small towns replete with onioned churches, larger than life brass statues in the Soviet Heroic mode dedicated to the dead of previous wars and the politicians who caused them. And a sprinkling of tanks and planes to underline the timeline.

These memorials are a far cry from the neat obelisks in English country villages. But then the scale of the slaughter was different. In Britain half a million soldiers and civilians lost their lives in WWII. In the former USSR twenty-seven million perished.

And now in a supermarket car park in a previously Closed City at the end of the day as lost as it is possible to be. Well, I am in the correct city, or so I believe. Messages and photographs by text are exchanged and I am instructed to stay where I am to wait for guidance which arrives in less than an hour.

A car pulls up and a woman alights wearing a parka to defeat the chill in the air calling out "Dereka?"

I smile, Anna smiles and I am hugged in the Russian style.

Another chase through ill lit cobbled city streets, slippery and ridged tramlines for the unwary, holes to be circumvented. In fifteen minutes we enter a courtyard through a massive arch which is part of a ubiquitous block apartment, and when I switch the engine off, calm, or at least quiet, descends.

Luggage removed, bike locked twice and covered and it's up these steps to the third floor without the aid of lift. I wondered where the man driving the car, whom I presumed to be a husband, had gone, not willing to carry panniers. The answer, it transpired, was not a husband but a taxi driver hired especially for the occasion of leading me across the city.

With no delay this female saviour showed me to my room and thence to the shower; no indoor banya here. Once clean, and re clothed in less dusty and slightly less dirty clothes I am sitting down to supper fighting off an enormous cat who is determined to share my large helping of fresh fried fish caught in the nearby river. I try to fend the cat off with cucumber but he is not stupid and continues the attack until his mistress feeds him from the pan.

Fed, watered and now relaxed with black tea served I can study this woman. She has a natural beauty; cheekbones are high and Russian, smooth brow, one blue eye and one brown both of which shine with curiosity and bright intelligence, straight nose and generous lips, the entirety framed with gleaming dark brown hair. I am, of course, an awestruck and enamoured fan for life; the more so when I learn that in this country she is a TV presenter of renown.

We talk of Mongolia and Siberia. We are sitting in south western Russia; my host has not yet travelled east of Moscow. But, she says, she will.

To sleep around midnight; tomorrow is a working day for Anna which could be why I find myself sharing with her and a man, a broad blue desk with accents of grey and red plastic, a hard light in my eyes and a countdown, counting down. So it's here and now on TV live, with nary a chance to prepare.

This interview, and my second chance of TV fame, while not as long as the first, has the same result. Failure….

My Russian is more or less non-existent and simultaneous translation not yet automatic or subtitled. Additionally, I am finding it hard not to giggle. Anna resplendent in short sleeved blouse, me in t-shirt, suntan and singular tattoo enhanced by broad red biker braces, hair and beard uncut for months; the counter-part male presenter is seated and viewed on camera wearing a smart suit jacket, shirt and tie. Whilst under the desk, shorts and flip flops as the aircon is not at its best.

In two weeks, my bicycling chum Paul will be sitting in the self-same seat, having met the same person. His fame lasted thirty seconds longer than mine as he was filmed cycling around the Yuri Gagarin monument over the Volga in Engels. And I believe he spoke Chinese on TV.

But not to worry re: fame as now on the street the power of TV, Facebook and Vkontakte.ru is displayed by people approaching and smiling and pointing. But no offers of money are made.

At the water's edge in the tent of a café/restaurant sited specially to see the bridge spanning the river, joined by a journalist girl friend of my host. We take coffee and cake and speak of the troubles of Russia. For my host and the journalist, the troubles are not, I think, too huge; for they have connections to the political machine.

Once the lack of free speech is accepted and corruption, if not welcomed, at least understood, a successful life can be achieved. Although I later learned, first hand and privately, of the pain that is involved.

The city is pleasant if tired at the margins. The commercial areas are, generally speaking, two storeys, turn of the century built in brick. Statues in the upper parts hiding in alcoves, many buildings painted with faded Mediterranean colour schemes of pink and green and cream and pale blue.

Some streets have colonnades of trees and pedestrianised roads. Which is a good thing, for drivers seem to think it is always open day for racing. Also in the central part of the city, single-storied domestic streets from the same time period; rougher and less kempt. Most are brick up to the windows, the upper half timber boarded, the whole grey with dust and age. And the ubiquitous corrugated tin roofs delivered from a central factory very far away.

They told me, for I did not know, that this is the hometown of Roman Arkadyevich Abramovich.

The city's favourite son began business life as a street trader and mechanic in a local factory before being jailed, a decade or so later, for theft and fraud counted in billions. Dollars, not roubles.

With convictions and lawsuits and ownership of a recruitment company specialising in hiring thugs for the protection of important people and subsequent quashing of court findings to become the owner of almost everything aluminium and big oil. At the age of thirty Mr. A became the confidant of President Yeltsin. So much so, that just three years later he dripped into the President's ear the name of a certain Mr Putin, the man, said Roman, who should be next in line to run Russia.

And so it came to pass.

Mr P became the biggest boss and Mr A bought the Chelsea Football Club and the Boss and sub-Boss stay best of friends forever.

For a city of less than a million, there appeared to be more than the average amount of political clout still reaching outward, upward and into the very next office to the highest power in the land.

I say the very next office as the man who ran that office also hailed from Saratov. And I am told this by another charming man taking coffee with me at the table of a different café, who just happened to be one of the richest criminals, now made legal, in the city.

I was meeting him because he was known to my host and the Director of an MBA driven Business School.

The Director, in her mid-thirties, was typical of the sleek and silken tall blondes possessed of a winning figure and smile, sharp mind, and confident with steeled determination who abound in certain layers of modern Russian society.

I was introduced to the Director because a software programme developed by my company could be of great value to Russian families with children. With attendant profits. But best sold with State approval.

The Director, at a cocktail reception the previous evening had understood concepts and money and murmured of joint enterprise and arranged the subsequent meeting.

State approval for the software of a new joint enterprise in Russia could be obtained said the man across the table. That the software was still in beta was not considered a problem; the joint enterprise could be backed by State funding. The profits shared with the real and actual owners of the State, not difficult.

All I had to do was to invest three million dollars US into the new joint venture, employ the gentleman as a consultant for disbursement of funds. Oh. And I had to make him famous.

In Russia, such things happen. The right contacts, the right place, the right time.

But he was infamous already. And I think, beyond my help. As I was, of his.

Due to the manufacturing of military aircraft, Mr Antonov, the now deceased but famous designer of aircraft being another of the hometown sons, Saratov was designated a Closed City until the early '90's. Being a Closed City meant that foreigners were simply not allowed to visit. Naturally the warrior, now retired, in me has always been interested in Closed Cities of the ex USSR

Unbeknownst I'd ridden through one in Siberia on the way south to Mongolia, Sibirsky on the road from Novosibirsk to Barnaul. Earlier still I was close to three more in Chelyabinsk and although Saratov was now open, three cities in the Oblast (region) are still closed. In all it is believed that fifty-nine Russian cities are still closed for military reasons.

Completely natural then to visit the evocatively named Saratov State Museum of Battle Glory, in Pobeda (Victory) Park. The park is huge; the military vehicles well maintained and impressive. What it doesn't show is the contribution made to the ex USSR of lend-lease equipment. The US, for example, sent 53% of all its wartime production of ammunition and ordnance to the Soviets.

In Britain, until 1941, we paid for US equipment in gold and when we ran out of gold gave them territories of the Empire. And until 1941 we charged the Russians, also in gold. From 1941 onwards Roosevelt, to appease his political critics, invented the Lend Lease system whereby the US lent equipment to the UK, USSR (and many other countries) interest free with materials to be returned when the war was over. Little was returned, or indeed expected, after the war.

The American support to the USSR from 1941 to 1945 was $11 billion, ($190 billion equivalent today). In the same period the US provided Britain $31 billion ($533 billion today) of war material. And the freedom of the Western world.

The UK debt was written down by 90%, and finally paid off to America and Canada in 2006. The Russians repaid their debt, also written down by 90%, of $700 million by 2006.

Here are some numbers in brief.

US & UK contribution to USSR war effort

Item	USA	UK
Trucks	427,284	
Combat vehicles	6,303	2,560
Motorcycles	35,170	1,721
Ordnance vehicles	2,328	
Petroleum Tons	2,670,371	
Foodstuffs tons	4,478,116	
Steam locomotives	1,911	
Diesel locomotives	66	
Flat cars	9,920	1,550
Dump cars	1,000	
Tank cars	120	
Ammunition	53%	
Pairs of boots		15,000,000
Anti-tank guns		5,000
Aircraft	14,833	7,000
Ships		27
Radar, radio & sonar		6,000
Aircraft engines		£1.15 bn
Ambulance		4,000
Tanks	7,000	6,606

Wikipedia. Table includes Canadian gifts within UK figures.

Obviously, Russians preferred Harleys. The table and my examples are simplified; it's hard to show like for like but it gives some idea. And it doesn't calculate the free exports from Russia to America of chrome and other precious metals

For political reasons, Soviet propaganda denied most of the aid during and after the war but when documents were recovered following the break-up of the USSR, Russian historian Boris Sokolov dismissed the often-cited Soviet figure of 4% Allied contribution of military aid under lend-lease as anywhere from 15% to 25% and in some cases upwards towards to 50%. America provided Russia with 53% of all the ammunition expended in the war.

The whole lend-lease issue is still a matter of controversy. And the ex USSR nations point to their twenty-seven million dead. What is the value of money against lives spent? Or value to the citizens of politicians deposed or kept in power?

But I'm walking round the War Park and looking for US or UK vehicles or equipment. I see none, about which I had no comment.

But I do see hordes of newly-weds getting wedding snaps taken.

With the worldwide interest in vintage and retro I've long realised that there is little Soviet period style clothing on offer although the market for Ural motorcycles and sidecars is evidently quite buoyant.

My commercial brain ticking, I jumped at the chance to visit the Museum of Yuri Gagarin. And there of course was the original brown leather jacket as worn by Yuri himself for the copying of and worldwide sale if copyrights can be obtained. No problem with the daughter of Mr Gagarin's wife, the wife now deceased and no mention of the alcoholism and other and numerous women in our hero's latter day career. Again the murmur, joint venture, investment in advance, all can be arranged. Declined, for now, by me.

Saratov's claim to all things Gagarin is interesting mainly because of the technical error that was a secret for many years. He attended the Saratov Industrial Technical School, studying tractors. Spent weekends training as a Soviet air cadet at a local flying club and earned extra money as a part-time dock labourer on the Volga River.

And here I'm exploring the museum on the site of the original technical school full of uniforms and photographs and general space bric a brac where the female attendant explained in awed tones that this was the handrail he'd actually touched when he climbed the stairs that I was climbing now. He left by rocket from Kazakhstan and landed by parachute in a field just across the Volga.

Because of technical problems, some still secret, the space craft and parachute landed on track but three hundred kilometres short of the zone. The fact is recorded that Anikhayat Takhtarova and her five-year-old granddaughter Rumiya, were planting potatoes in a field near the village of Smelovka when Gagarin walked up, still in space suit and helmet to introduce himself with a smile and Hello.

Smelovka is near Engels which is just over the river from Saratov where I went to see the brand-new building with monument attached, dedicated to his flight and opened by Russia just a month before I arrived. I ignored the tour, scooped up a handful of dirt from the field, which I still have today.

The dirt I have stolen is not reported in my luggage or at customs and neither is it for sale. It seems there are no deals for me to be done in Saratov; but not from the want of trying.

After my ignominious exit from Kazakhstan I knew that on re-entering Russia I need to get my passport stamped by the authorities to show I am registered once more as a temporary visitor.

For a private citizen to sponsor this might bring the unwanted attention of police, customs and other arms of the law. So, to a hotel that is known to provide extra-curricular services and for ten dollars US I hand over my passport to be collected, stamped, in the morning.

Which I do the next morning, early, and then forward to visit Anna's ship, left to her in her father's will.

Moored on the Volga, steel built, welded plates and a wooden deck, twenty metres long, seven metres at the beam, and I'm at a loss to try and classify its use. The superstructure and wheel house is forward at the bow, unlike fishing boats that steer from the rear. The ship is white, perhaps for camouflage in winter ice, and the superstructure, derricks and transom smartly painted yellow.

Nonplussed I remain and we go to visit another friend with a large motor cruiser and off down river to an island and barbecue café with delicious shashlik and fresh river fish served with beer if you want or fine Italian coffee and an explanation offered for the size of Anna's father's ship. This river, the Volga, further downstream, is forty-five kilometres wide from shore to shore. Wider in fact, than the channel of sea that separates my Island from the continent of Europe. You need a big ship, even for fishing.

And I accept with humility just how huge this country is.

The motorcycle's front tyre has now been replaced and the repairer is taking Anna and me to a biker café that she didn't know existed. Here is Saratov's answer to the Ace café. Russian rock 'n' roll pounds from a juke box, paraphernalia of all kinds for sale. Leather jackets, waistcoats adorned with club insignia, blue denim jeans and boots. I am greeted as a minor celebrity; Facebook and VKontake.ru have paved the way; the MBA school posting five times a day. Overwhelming and strange, all in a language I cannot speak.

The morning of the day before I'm due to leave; there is another moment of emotional upheaval waiting to rock my body and mind.

As the sun lifts we are driving slowly in Anna's car on a beaten up and pot-holed road that hugs the river north.

A village with tracks of dust and steep banks, cottages of weather blackened timber, intricately carved window frames faded, painted blue or white but no smoke from the chimneys nor wires attached to the telegraph poles and for the most part devoid of human activity. To a cottage with tin-roofed poor sheds attached and goats and single cow. "This," Anna tells me, "is where I came as a child to collect the milk each day."

There are children here, hair unkempt, and an ill-dressed Babushka. When I look at the photograph later I am the only one smiling for the lens.

We drive on. Her father's cottage viewed, two storeys, walls bulging and collapsing outward with no reason for repair in the village that has died.

Through a forest of birch up a hill and onto a cliff with a good view of the river in the valley.

I step out of the car and walk to the edge looking down into the valley, the river shining and the village clinging to the bank

Emotion is on me as I think of the journey that Anna has told me in the car. From this small, desolate and dusty village to school and local college; because of her beauty becoming the possession of a gangster and then escaping to the capital where her good looks, good nature, smile and sharp mind lift her to television fortune and then, beaten by the superficiality of the capital and the rarefied loneliness of fame retreating to her home city, a quieter life, peace and assistance to her ageing mother.

These people, these Russians. It takes but one step and an outstretched hand

and you can, if you wish, have new and very dear friends for life.

These Russians. The villages are empty, they've fled to the cities. But they have great education, good prospects and opportunity abounds. The Oligarchs and Politicians rape and corrupt the country, but the people still live their lives.

These Russians. Warm, friendly, great good humour. The West, through fear, treats them with disdain, the fear is mutual and mirrored back. In truth, they do not need the West.

These Russians, two years later applauding Mr Putin for starting the war in Ukraine and stealing Crimea. Such is the power of propaganda.

Emotion is flooding and there are tears wet on my cheeks as I say goodbye to the river below, goodbye to the ancient village on the river bank hard by the birch forest, good bye to the friends I have made in the city and the dachas.

In the morning, I am led by a biker met in the café, out to the city limits. With a high wave and wide smile, he peels away and I leave on the road heading west passing the 'Church of the Icon of the Mother of God Soothe My Sorrows in Saratov'. How apt, I thought, when Google translated the phrase.

CENTURIES
OF BLOOD

Anna has called ahead with an introduction to the family of her journalist friend, who live in the small town of Liski, five hundred kilometres west of Saratov on the road to the border at Sumy.

To find the house in the town I am speaking to Anna on my mobile phone with the illegal Russian sim card. She is speaking to the parents of her friend on a separate phone and together I'm guided to the door of a wooden cottage painted green with windows in blue frames and the suntanned silver haired host in white t-shirt and black nylon running trousers standing out on the porch with a welcome. And then of course I must park the bike at the back of house, in deep gravel, for the prevention of theft.

The first words are to direct me to the banya at the bottom of the garden.

I am not affronted; it has been a long and dusty ride although my wax jacket, washed by machine in Saratov, is now a pretty pale hunting pink and to my eyes at least, quite clean.

The water for the shower in the banya is gravity fed from an oil drum perched on the roof, heated by the sun. I shower, feel better and put the same clothes back on.

As befits the parents of a journalist my hosts are knowledgeable of the area.

Over a meal of grey meat and vegetables covered in seasoned flour and fried, I discovered that the town was renamed Georgiu-Dezh in 1965 to honour the Romanian communist leader, Gheorghe Gheorghiu-Dej. Something went wrong I think, about which I know not, and it was renamed back to Liski twenty-five years later.

This land is steeped in blood. To the west, the family tell me, is the city of Belogrod through which I will travel tomorrow. The Oblast was awarded the

Order of Lenin, the city was awarded the Order of the Patriotic War and just five years previously was bestowed the honorary title, City of Military Glory. And we in the West wonder why Mr Putin, creator of more wars, is so popular amongst his countryman.

In 1944 in a village called Prokhorovka just north of Belgorod, a fierce battle was fought involving one thousand three hundred tanks and heavy armoured vehicles. The Soviets claim it was the largest ever tank battle in history. Perhaps it is because the Soviets won. Operation Barbarossa, which they lost in 1941, involved two thousand tanks in one battle, and six thousand overall. Victors write history.

This land was fought over the by White and Red armies during the Russian Revolution. It was fought over by the Germans in World Wars I & II.

It is no longer surprising to me, of emotions disturbed, when I speak to Ukrainians of Russia. For a week, in 1919, Belgorod was the temporary capital city of Ukraine, deep inside today's Russia.

Blood is still spilt here. In the year after my passage, on April 22, 2013, a mass shooting occurred on a street in Belgorod. The gunman, Sergey Pomazun opened fire with a semi-automatic rifle on several people at a gun store and on a sidewalk, killing six people. During his apprehension, he stabbed a policeman. He was sentenced to life in prison on August 23, 2013.

But now, having had coffee at a petrol station fill-up and a hearty breakfast of the undetermined remains of last night's supper thoughtfully wrapped in grease proof paper and placed in a paper bag for eating on the road, I am passing the city discussed previously with no stops for museums or war parks on the final five hundred kilometres of my journey through Russia.

And here's the thing. This land, blood soaked from the Middle Ages onwards, fought over by the Khans, Lithuanians and later the Poles then owned by Ukrainian Cossacks for one hundred and fifty years before the civil war, at the border with the same language spoken on each side where no official appears overtly concerned over the loss of half of my ownership documents and I'm through in an hour and on a potholed Ukrainian village road near Pokrovka, dust rising pink in the sunset with the twin blue cupolas of a very grand church dominating all. But my mind is less fearful and the body relaxed as I search for a ten-dollar hotel.

Which, as it's the border, cost me twenty-five.

To Kyiv in the morning, five hundred kilometres of the widest horizons, some forest, tin roofed villages where the well is still used, petrol stations manned by people who smile; it is good to be back, here in Ukraine.

I've phoned ahead with an ETA and I'm to be taken to a party – a birthday of a friend and a welcome for me, returned from the wilds.

Into the city and I know, by the familiarity of the holes and craters and ruts in the roads, more or less where I am. To the apartment of my business partner, showered, clean clothes and the luxury of being transported in her car to a restaurant of renown meeting friends I haven't seen for some years.

A most enjoyable evening. The party girl is Natalie's best friend. A diminutive but extraordinarily attractive woman, Vika surrounds me with perfume and swirling brilliant blonde hair; kisses to both cheeks twice and full body hugs and insists that I sit on her right.

The table for twenty is large, the menu in English, but my choices, when served, look like a different language. If I had as much wine as my fellow guests I wouldn't have worried. And in truth

I'm not because the evening is full of laughter and love.

On the following day, we are in the garden of the dacha that belongs to my business partner's mother in law where we collect ripe fruit in large enamel bowls. The bowls are white, with blue lining at the lip, the occasional chip showing their vintage.

Shining red apples, yellowing pears, grapes still green but delicious and dark red cherries, plentiful red currants weighing down the branches. And though now out of season there are a few strawberries still, and melons at ground level. There are vegetables to be harvested too; ruby red peppers both Bulgarian and Chili, tomatoes in a range from yellow through green to red, aubergines in customary purple. They are picked for fresh eating, but most for preservation; fruit turned into jam and the vegetables pickled for the lean months ahead.

The car is loaded, the fruit and vegetables decanted to plastic bags or five litre jars and we're off back to the city. Cyclists of both genders are out on the village roads, the young in shorts and the babushkas in summer frocks with cardigans crammed in baskets. At a railway crossing a maroon vintage Dnieper Twin with sidecar attached is stopped waiting for a line of rusting oil tank freight cars to pass. In the late afternoon sun the rusting tankers display a range of colours from chemicals spilled as wide and deep as the harvest we've collected.

And I'm reminded that the days are a tiny bit shorter and with the harvest, Summer is running into Autumn and my home is still two thousand kilometres more to the west.

Late on Wednesday afternoon and the door-bell is buzzing long and loud.

Natalie's mother answers the telephone intercom, but the answering voice is in English, not understood. Natalie to the phone, whoop of surprise and she's out of the door, down to the ground floor to meet my travel mate Paul. Who is invited in, with his bike in the lift, up to the apartment and his bravery and grit admired by all.

This man, of whom I am in awe, has just ridden thirteen thousand kilometres to arrive at the door.

A feast provided by Natalie's mother and we crowd around the table to listen to his tales. Of sleeping in ditches, on floors. Of riding in mountains, through rivers, deserts and crossing five borders where English is not spoken. We exchange notes on short lived TV stardom; he brings love from mutual friends in the East.

And all too soon to sleep in a room which we share. This time we have a bed each, not a trestle or the floor.

A few more words about Paul, about the future he's riding towards. He made it home in the last days of September to be met, fresh from the Ferry, by his family and friends. He rode the final forty-five kilometres to his village, the last five with his father on his own bike alongside and was astonished to find flags and the bunting and people lining the streets to cheer and wave and welcome him home. He'd raised £15,000 for charity having ridden fifteen thousand kilometres. Two weeks later, having waited for his son's return, his father died in peace. Paul and his father, two modest, unassuming and wonderfully strong men.

Here in Kyiv I'm in Petrovka, a region with a huge vibrant market of small stalls all under cover. Each stall is a timber framed three metres by two with lock up steel frontage.

The market is full of new and used books and vinyl records, high quality clothing for men and women, boots and shoes, mops, buckets and brooms made from twigs. If it's clothing you want the stall holder pulls round a small curtain where would be buyers balance on one leg to try things on. Accompanied by giggles.

It's also famed for being the best place in the country for the purchase of pirate software and music. Or was, until the Tax Authorities raided. Not because the product was pirated and illegal, but because the stall holders were not paying their tax.

Opposite Petrovka is Gorodok, a large mall, for which Natalie was the senior project manager with birthday girl Vika as Director of Money for the entire period of construction. The holding company and its Directors became rich and later arrested. Natalie and Vika did neither.

And opposite Gorodok is a dealer of Piaggio who had been entrusted with the full service of the Stelvio. A change of oils, checking and adjustment of valve clearances and to include hooking it up to their computer. Which they did and declared it tickety-boo.

For some reason this wasn't as exciting as the service in the lock up garage in Kazakhstan. And they didn't check the tightness of nuts and bolts, thus causing loud consternation in the next country two days later.

Finally in Kyiv I've been to my office in the centre of the city, showed the crew some pictures of my journey to which they dutifully ooohed and ahhhed and as I'd signed all the documents that needed signing and I'm released, like an errant schoolboy, to get back on the road.

A special delivery, personal to me, has been made. Back in Saratov I'd called the DVLA, the British vehicle licensing authority and explained that half of my ownership document had disappeared. The empathetic man to whom I spoke sent out a copy to my home that very day. With no charge. Then my wife forwarded it onward, signed for post, to my office for collection.

Now legal and peeling around the ring road at dawn to beat the traffic, bear right and I'm on the road to

Zhytomyr and Rivne and the border at Krakovets.

I call in to check out the motorcycle mechanics at Motorush and we're out for a few beers on the town, celebrating my safe passage so far. Well… they're sinking beers, I'm drinking Coke, but it's fun and great company and we swap motorcycle stories as I re-live the experience under the bus.

One last brush with law as I cruised the next day on spanking new tarmac on a road now uprated to motorway. Outside the town of Novoiavorivsk I was, in truth, speeding more than the limit. So, when the short and chubby cop waved me down with his white tipped baton, I pulled up on the central reservation. Why make it easy I thought. Off with the helmet, slap on a smile and my hand outstretched for hello.

"You speed." he said, but he had no technical proof. No radar gun, just his feeling, correct in this case. Sauntering around the bike he confirmed I was an Anglia in a hurry to get home.

"Protocol." I say. "Pay Bank?" he says. I smile, "Yes please."

He smiles too, knowing this is going nowhere.

"Which football?" to which I answered "Manchester" because I only knew two teams and he probably hadn't heard of Arsenal. Then I went into a brand-new mime, never tried by me before.

"Дочка have дитина" said I, which, for non-Ukrainian speakers means Daughter have Baby. And I mimed a big stomach then indicated forward speed for me. "Ahh!" he cried. "Good roads, go!"

Whether he thought I was having a daughter, or my wife or my daughter was having a baby was not truly material to the circumstance. But there was no fine, or bribe to be paid and I was off once more and riding. With a tad less gusto.

At the border, no-one questioned my brand-new documents but Polish

Customs were concerned that I was smuggling fuel. I stand at their window, wearing my helmet to prove I'm not driving a truck and explaining that the tank takes only fifteen litres. And anyway, I'd forgotten to fill up with petrol that's cheaper than theirs.

But the plastic luggage must be opened, for guns and drugs to be found, which is not simple due to the amount of duct tape that swathes each one. I look at the duct tape, I look at the officer. He looks at me, then at the tape and says "Open it please. All."

Tape is ripped off, cases undone, tools, coffee filters and dirty clothes spill-out across the floor. Stuffed back in when the Officer nods to repeat the process twice more. Branded Duct tape had run out in Kazakhstan and the replacement roll I bought there is cheap stuff, not really thick or sticky. So everything has to be duct-wrapped twice to keep the sides closed together and the water out.

Clear of customs I stop on the road to make sure all is ship-shape and secure. There seems to be more tape than plastic now, including the wodge around the hand guards and the strips securing the Satnav/Phone and its now semi-waterproof holder.

With the Sim card changed from Russian to English I am in receipt of a text. My daughter is to give birth to a baby in a few days.

Be careful of the lies you tell and the prayers you offer up….

Mid-afternoon and I'm on the forecourt of a petrol station near Tarnow wrestling with the rear fender. A bolt, not checked by Piaggio's men in Kyiv, had loosened and fallen out; the fender shifted round the wheel and had been grinding and scraping the road. Like all modern petrol stations the world over they sold nail varnish, hard liquor, coffee and petrol but nothing useful for a motorcyclist looking for a saw. Eventually, sprawled underneath, I managed to jury rig the fender with a plastic tie. I was pleased, for carrying the plastic ties for twenty thousand kilometres was justified at last.

I hadn't found a motorway yet and roads here are slow, as the towns and villages continuously merge with a maximum speed of sixty. No wonder Polish bikers ride with insanity attached to their brains.

Onward then, spinning forward as fast as I dare to find a motorway near Krakow and crazy high speed tag with cars behind me flashing lights to move over and overtake even faster. Past Katowice and Wroclaw when, searching for petrol and off the main road I came over a hill and spied a motel on the right.

The motel was near to closing and they quoted a price for the night. They weren't up for much a haggle for Euros in cash but gave me ten percent off with breakfast now included.

And the chef went back to the kitchen and knocked up steak and chips.

Very early in the morning I passed on the ever-present cucumber and sliced tomatoes, ate sausage, ham and egg and bread and three cups of coffee and out and onto to the bike and no more stops for customs and borders.

I started very early to avoid the traffic going west. But naturally thousands of others thought the same so joining the rush it was over the unmanned border, through and then Dresden again and Leipzig, and slower in the mountains at Kassel where spray from recent rain cuts visibility to five metres and finally into Bochum where I cannot find the address or phone of Birgit.

Enquiries made for a room at the Acorra but eighty-five euros is too rich for my taste and pocket so it's on to the Ibis, near the station, which is cheaper but small, gloomy and the internet is broken.

The night porter arrives with reluctance and a new password for the internet and a suggestion to call the helpline. To which I reply what sort of hotel charges nine euros for the internet that does not work; I have it taken off the bill.

In the morning I leave without breakfast, a dog in a roll at a petrol station later is sustenance enough and in the early afternoon, two more languages under my wheels, I am parked a day early in the car park for the Ferry. Tomorrow's ticket for a sailing at eight in the evening was not, "No Sir." just not acceptable here.

Into the office to buy a new ticket for today, to find the price four times more than what I'd already paid. A kindly employee took me aside and pointed to an internet connection. "Buy it on there," she said, "online." So I did, for just twice the price of the ticket in hand and was up the metal ramp once more, bike lashed down and me across three seats falling asleep until we dock at Dover.

Then Petrol.

And Home.

EPILOGUE

There was no band or ticker tape or bunting waiting outside my house

But here, now, I'm safe and that is more than enough. A kiss on the lips and the feel of soft skin of the cheek, inhaling the fragrance of love and long warm hug of greeting and a cup of English Breakfast tea with milk, sipped slowly in quiet satisfaction of a good journey over and safe return to home.

Except, and just two days later, I'm dad-dancing on a painful foot around the kitchen with the news that we are grandparents for the very first time.

In the notebook that I carry with me, I had written, on the ferry home, that after Kazakhstan I'd say never again.

But the fear and the pain have gone and I'm left, still, with much emotion and memories of the people I met.

Fabulous without exception, I would like to meet them all again.

I can ride very long distances. In a day, or month, or longer. I can pick myself up when I fall, suffer breaks in bones and continue going forward.

But I can only do this when sustained by the love of family and close friends. Denied close proximity of love over distance and time I know that I am susceptible to emotional challenge; fear rises, judgement warps.

But not today.

I am content. And will be, until the Spring.

ADDENDUM

I took a little time to decide on the motorcycle and the kit. It's not germane to the main stories, but you may find my struggle helpful if you are searching for bikes or kit for yourself.

Before the Off

Back in 2011, I met a man in a motorway car park. He was a little younger than me and rode a tall and upright BMW of some kind. He wore a clean, shiny, insipid beige suit of textile; had GPS mounted on the bars and blue tooth everything, everywhere.

In short, he looked like a thoroughly zipped up modern motorcyclist, albeit without much élan or style, whilst I was wearing black leather, old jeans and a ripped T-shirt, the epitome of a hard-ass rocker.

We made conversation about his bike; it transpired he used to ride a Harley, but now he was made new and reconfigured as an Adventure Rider.

The fact that he admitted he'd never left the UK or ridden more than four hundred kilometres in a day on either bike was neither here nor there and probably normal; but a worm had entered my brain.

Three months earlier I'd returned to England having ridden my sleek but ageing cherry red Victory Vegas cruiser on a trip from London to Kurdistan and the borders of Iran, Iraq and Syria. I couldn't cross into those countries as I had planned no specific route other than an easterly heading. I had no visas. But I'd travelled in the Caucasus mountains of Armenia and Georgia, taken selfies with Mt. Ararat as a backdrop and covered thousands of kilometres on roads that most would consider off.

Now, in the carpark looking at the man, I wanted to be an Adventure Rider. No matter that I'd just ridden eighteen thousand kilometres in Mr Schott's finest black leather jacket and Levi jeans. I knew I couldn't be a Real Adventurer until I did it on an Adventure Motorcycle. With Adventure Clothing to match.

A Parallel Universe

I have an addictive and, some say, an obsessional personality. With the help of an amazing twelve step programme, I have remained clean and sober for thirty years; but the personality traits survive.

Hence the worm in my brain had grown into a hissing serpent of endless jealousy as I read performance data on machines and travel gear.

With increasing fervour I had joined half a dozen web forums, read every feedback, review and complaint written over the last two years. A stack of motorcycle magazines, not unlike the leaning tower of Pisa, grew at the side of my bed.

Consideration was given to height, size and weight and discarded immediately thereon although I did want to go European.

Japanese bikes are reliable, solid and good to ride; where was the fun in that?

Euro-proven were Beemers, KTM who failed, for fear of failure, to back Charley and Ewan on their rides; Ducatis were a bit too fast and flighty, Triumph still proving the opposite.

The choice of The Chosen One didn't take that long really. Just a couple of month's intensive research before the bike was located, negotiated and paid for.

But hear this and raise your hands to heaven my equally obsessive friends – I bought the bike just before Christmas. And ten days later it was still unseen.

It couldn't be a BMW of course. I'd watched Charley and Ewan crossing continents dressed like the carpark man. Or perhaps they beat him to it. I loved their courage and humour, but none of the style. Estate agents tell of giving advice to homeowners with houses to sell; go bland they say, paint all in Magnolia. But I was off to Mongolia, bland would not do at all.

I had arranged, for January 3rd, to pick

up the bike between 11.00 and 12.00. According to Google maps the journey time by car to Wareham, Dorset was one hour and fifty-five minutes. We would need to leave at nine thirty to arrive at the appointed time.

Only the true obsessive will understand the act of supreme control exercised when, sitting in the passenger seat of my wife's car at 09.47 I was told that we would have to get petrol first.

Why hadn't this been done the night before? Maybe get the car serviced and change the tyres all round before we go? Stop at Mc Donald's for a sausage-egg McMuffin. A what??? I sat smiling, nodding, teeth gritted.

Training paid off; slow down, think calm thoughts. I even paid for the petrol and whilst there bought a motorcycle newspaper to get me through the next two hours.

A calm of sorts descended until the ringing of mobile phone. "Unknown number" said the dial. I knew immediately it was a client, and I knew, because it said "Unknown" exactly who the client was.

He was having a problem. He did not know of my problem, which was much greater than his. My problem was that he was calling me on Motorcycle Collection Day when I was actually on The Journey. I solved the problem with two international and one domestic phone call and reverted to reading. I was using controlled breathing by now: calm, breathe, calm, breathe. If she noticed, my wife said nothing.

Then we were lost, five hundred metres from my goal. I had no GPS or map. I was relying on Google on my phone. Unreliable postcodes and policeman were consulted. Hither, thither and more hither.

Finally, at two minutes before noon, Dorset Bikes.

I stepped inside the store, stopped and all but fell to my knees. Huge. Black.

Shiny. The Stelvio, hand built in Mandello del Lario by much talented engineers, gleamed and I smiled back.

A thousand hours of research and here I stood at the beginning of a brand-new rainbow.

Into the silence of my deep and profound contemplation noise entered.

"Derek?"

The owner of Dorset Bikes, veteran biker and all round wizard Ivan brought me gently back and connected me to Earth, 2012.

A cup of tea in my hand, I sat at his desk, papers to sign. My wife, unaffected by this display of unworldly goings on, smiled and sipped her tea too. She patted the Stelvio's seat as one might gentle a horse.

But Ivan wasn't finished with me yet.

He'd magicked up and fitted a pair of HID headlights. Lights on. New cans on the exhaust. Engine on. Vroom. Like a two-wheeled celestial chariot the Stelvio shone, quivered and snorted bass power.

The engine turned off, I approached the beast nervously. Nervous because the seat was about a metre high and I have the legs of a short rhinoceros. I had them wheel the bike outside.

With both hands gripping my thigh firmly I swung it over the saddle, slid forward and tilted the two hundred and thirty kilos upright as I went. Toes scrabbling for purchase on the road I managed to stabilise myself and the machine.

Sean, Ivan's outstanding mechanical genius, gave me a fifteen second briefing on how to turn on the heated handgrips and switch between menus on the on-board computer and that was it.

Switch on, lights on, engine on, in gear, moving, feet up, moving, gear up, turn right, turn right, gear up, feed a little more power. Hmmm. I can see over these cars. Slowing at roundabout, slide forward on seat, gear down, down, clutch in, toes on ground. Hmmm, ok. I can do this...

Gaining confidence, I followed my wife's car at around one hundred and twenty kph on the motorway with a reluctance, it seemed for advancing faster. I wondered if this was the infamous flat spot I had read about. Meantime I was running low on petrol so I overtook said wife, indicated and pulled into the service area to fill up.

My wife agreed it was not worth waiting and carried on ahead. I filled up – still trying to get used to digital petrol gauge – paid and set off.

As I pulled out of the services the bike started to cough and wouldn't respond to the throttle. I tried each gear and various levels of acceleration but it just got worse. After four or five kilometres I stopped and called Ivan who transferred me, fast, to Sean. Who said all he could of think of was that the petrol, somehow mixed with dirt in the tank – but asked if could I get it back to the shop?

I was almost exactly midway in the journey. Go forward to home was ninety kilometres and back at some future date, or get another one hundred kilometres onto the tyres today. You guessed; no contest.

I set off with the bike coughing and accelerating and slowing independent of anything I did with the throttle. Up and down hills was hard; if I didn't overtake I would slow down even more. When I did overtake, who knew if the revs would stay high enough to pass. A challenge but later, and only in retrospect, great fun.

Sean rode half a mile and returned leading with an embarrassed smile. Then checked both plugs, discarded one and replaced; and the HT lead too for good measure. A test to be taken and back in ten minutes.

"What speed did you do?" he asked with a grin. I told him, about one hundred and twenty kph.

"Hmm, who did this then?" he said with a grin. There on the trip recorder, one hundred forty and two point three.

That'll do. And with thanks and goodbyes again I wound back through the village roads, the dual carriageway and finally the motorway. Same roads, different bike.

It was raining now. Pouring. But the bike was perfectly balanced and held a line at two or ninety through bends. I noticed not the rain – I had a windscreen now, the first in my biking life; the rain did not touch me – it simply shone like a million diamonds as the HID lights cleaved a path through the traffic. A glorious throaty roar developed as the Vtwin sang - and to my astonishment the speed gauge showed three high digits.

My world had changed, I had slipped into a Parallel Universe of effortless travel.

This experience of a windshield – no wind tearing arms out of sockets. Smooth power – not arm wrenching like my Vmax, just on and ever on… I could even hear opera playing from my Bluetooth helmet at high speed.

The journey home was far too quick. And having arrived, I was not allowed out again that night.

All that I did later, with good foresight I think, was to add crash-bars round the engine, hand-sprayed fetchingly in red.

CHANGING GEAR

The motorcycle world is as complex as any other grouping within human society. Cruiser, crotch-rocketeer, vintage, enduro, trials and commuters.

Each sub section has its own mores, myths and, yes, dress code. Motorcyclists are divided by special interests, unified by the camaraderie of riding two wheels.

The average biker (if there were such a person) would say he or she is not interested in how they look, it's just about the ride. But each and every one does make an effort to identify with their part of the tribe. And once off the bike, they form up like troops. The cruiser crowd are in black leather jackets, crotchateers wear multi-coloured leather onesies just like their race track heroes, and then all the way up, or down, to commuters and adventurers in textiles.

All of this makes it patently obvious that I could not be a fully-fledged and proper sitting upright RTW (Round the World) type of rider unless I was correctly attired. A century and a half ago no-one would dream of adventuring anywhere without a pith helmet. So it is today.

It started with the man in the carpark and moved up a gear when I read Adventure Bike Rider, a magazine with tales of intrepid derring do from long distance motorcyclists criss-crossing the world on giant BMW adventure bikes. The specialist bikes, the clothing, the roads, oh, just everything. I was enthralled - I wanted to be one.

It took me a couple of days to realise that, actually, I was one of these derring do-ers. But I was doing it on a cruiser wearing outlaw style black leathers. The voices in my head started up. "Well you don't look like a derring do-er. Wrong bike, wrong clothes. No derring."

One of the voices, a sensible one, said "Lookit. Every other RTW (Round

The World) does it on a Beemer. They couldn't do it on great grunty cruisers."

This voice was answered by a sneakier one "Yes, but they loooook like RTW's." Rejoindered with "As do half the commuters riding to work."

At this point I was laying on the floor trying to wrench my head off - you know what I mean, you've been there yourself. So to appease my voices I got up and started more research.

By now I knew exactly which features the best Adventure Textile Jackets had: in which conditions the various zip in / zip out features are best used; whether a 3/4 jacket is better than hip length and which technical trousers will fit with what.

I also knew riveting things like the three-layer system and why merino wool is best next to the skin.

But this is a tale of capricious choice, and biker stuff bores non-bikers.

With the research almost completed I had decided (which means obsessed over for weeks) on a shiny olive coloured confection from Lindstrands - a famous Swedish manufacturer of Adventure clothing. I had tried the jacket, but not the trousers, at the Motorcycle Live 2011 exhibition.

The Swedish gentleman who helped me through the painful decision process "I would like a jacket that will serve me well in both the desert and high mountains" was assiduous in detailed attention. Never once did he try to sell me a thing; simply analysed my needs and showed me exactly what was needed to survive the journey.

I did not completely believe him of course. So I bought nothing. But on my return and over the next few days once more I researched every site and knowledgeable magazine I could find. Every source confirmed what he said. A little more research and the retail outlet was sorted (and visited for more try-ons although it was an internet warehouse that did not generally deal with the public) and the price sorted. Lindstrands Olive, perfection and the epicentre of my desire.

My wife is good with me, but not so much with motorcycles and obsessional behaviour. She knows little of motorcycling arcana, and prefers to remain in blissful ignorance of the finer details of Outlast and Thermal Pile.

So how come she bought me a lilac coloured all season Belstaff motorcycle textile adventure jacket for Christmas?

E-bay has a lot to answer for.

I had decided just then that olive green was not the colour to match a red and black motorcycle. With this revelation and in less than a nanosecond I searched and found Belstaff. An English brand you may think; well yes. And no.

Belstaff was bought, backed and made famous by an illustrious Italian Movie Mogul. Who saw the Steve McQueen connection and projected the brand directly into the Hollywood A list. And me.

E-bay. Belstaff. Lilac.

The man in the car park and Ewan and Charley might wear Belstaff, but they didn't have the balls for Lilac.

Click.

"Darling, you know you were thinking about a Christmas present for me?"

I hope they like Lilac in Ulaan Bator.

A month passes. I am proudly upright riding a black and red Italian Adventure Motorcycle and see myself in a store's plate glass window astride the machine in technical Lilac. Black, red and lilac?

The stylista synapses shrieked into life. "No, no, no. It must be a red jacket. With black jeans."

There are brands, wannabees and pure rubbish.

At the top of the tree I had already discovered Belstaff and Barbour. Barbour invented the whole wax jacket thing, and it was they who clothed Mr

McQueen. Although it is said he wore both brands back then, in the day.

Truth is both companies offered the same base fabric, manufactured in Britain by The British Millerain Company. The Miller family (Miller Rain, geddit?) started in 1880 exporting today specialist fabrics worldwide. Including China where Barbour, Belstaff and the wannabees are made.

Anyway, this wannabee RTW was not going to be satisfied with a same old, same old, common or garden variety of Belstaff or Barbour, oh no! Or even a wannabee wax jacket motorcycling jacket.

I went back to the roots of wax jackets and found Carl Wilson's Claymore Jacket company just up the Calder Valley from the Millerain factory.

So when I said to Carl, "Can I have a wax cotton biker jacket in red?", he said "Yes. Of course."

Thus Carl and his elves (or elvettes) individually designed and made to my measurements a ten ounce Millerain deep red waxed cotton motorcyclist jacket. A perfect fit.

I bought some very good boots. Made in Minnesota by the Chippewa company. Black to match the Australian black Kevlar jeans but I'd almost sent them back when looking again on the Net to confirm I'd made a great purchase I realised the site of the man who recommended them so highly, was a boot and black leather fetishist.

No matter. The Chippewa Boot Company call them the Fireman boot; I liked them because they had laces and a zip up front – so much quicker to get on or off than with any other I own. And comfortable right from the off.

So now I had both the motorcycle and the kit.

And then, of course, I rode to Mongolia.

A Digression on Bribes

As a digression, here's what you should know about traffic cops in the countries of the former Soviet Union.

The role of traffic police is well known and has little to do with controlling traffic; the primary role is to extort bribes to supplement their miserable salaries.

And corruption amongst traffic police in new EU countries – Bulgaria and Croatia I can personally attest to – is still rife.

On my first visit to Ukraine on a motorcycle I was stopped by the infamous traffic police three times within one hundred and fifty kilometres of the border. Each stop cost me ten euros for the advice to slow down or don't undertake or whatever reason they could pluck out of the air. Of course, they told me the real fine was two hundred euros but if I paid cash now there would be a big discount....

In Ukraine and further east, the speed limit on a non-motorway roads is ninety kph; in a town sixty. The difficulty is knowing when you are in a town - or village - and when you're on a main road. Most are equally potholed or otherwise churned up so you can't tell the difference.

The rule is that when you enter a town or village the town sign means you are in the limits, speed is sixty kph. When you leave the town the name board has a red line through it. However, you can ride for ten kilometres or more with no sign of habitation whatsoever or find villages are joined together one after another.

The New EU.

In the new EU countries, there is not much to be done because they only stop you for genuine violations. The switch sell, if it happens, is when they start telling you must surrender your plastic licence to them, go to the nearest town and make a bank to bank transfer to the Police Authority and bring a receipt of payment from the bank back to them at the point they have stopped you.

To which you would normally say "Oh dear, is there something we can do on a more local basis?" They'll make you an offer but because you're in the EU the shakedown is going to cost €30 to €50.

However, the smart answer is "Yes Officer I will do that – here is my licence".

You can do this because you had the foresight to garner three licences from the DVLA before you left home. And the DVLA will let you get more licences on line so you can stay topped up.

Hand over the licence. Go.

How to avoid paying bribes when you are stopped.

There are two parts to this. The first is the more important.

When you are stopped, get off your bike, take off your helmet, walk toward them with a smile and hold out your hand to shake theirs. This show of international friendship is so alien they may well just look around your bike, ask which football team you support and say, "Nice bike, go."

The next thing is that they will ask you to get in their car. This is so they can make their pitch out of the weather and away from any bike mounted cameras or recording devices you may have switched on. So, try not to get in the car and if you do, record all that is said as openly as you can.

They will pull out a sheaf of documents and start to fill them in. This form is the 'protocol' which is the document to record your transgression and will be placed before the court, when you go to court. Amazingly almost every traffic violation, or so the police would have you believe, has a fine of €200 or more. At some point during the form completion they are going to say the magic words "€200" whereupon you suck in your breath and they say, well… how much money have you got with you?

The going rate is €20 which seems quite reasonable until you are stopped five times in a day.

To avoid the fine or the upcoming bribe, you say, with a smile, "Protokol pazhalsta." Which means give me the protocol please and implies you want to go to court to settle this. You know you're not going to court, they know you're not going to and that they have no redress on an intra-national basis.

Traffic police cannot arrest you into custody for a traffic violation; they cannot ask for payment of a fine which you pay into a bank, you cannot be stopped at an international border for a traffic violation. So, if you insist on the protocol and keep smiling they will normally let you go. Should they ever go as far as issuing the protocol, write on it (it's in duplicate) "I do not understand what the officer number (from their badge) is saying."

I offer this advice from experience. But I am not a lawyer so don't even think of trying to sue.

My personal experience is that apart from Georgia, where they fired the whole force overnight and replaced them with more ethical and better trained graduates, the cops in the former USSR are still underpaid and still extort bribes to make up their salary to a living wage.

Authors note: This was correct in 2012 but in 2014 in Ukraine the traffic police were disbanded and some better incorruptible people hired. However, you should still heed the road signs.

ACKNOWLEDGEMENTS

Grateful thanks to all the friends who gave their time to help shape this book.

Amongst them, Agnieska Wiklo, Duncan Gough, Eloise Smith, Imogen Mansfield-Keane, James Hydzik,, Keith Pearce, Natalie Rastabarova, Olga Popova for her fresh design ideas, and, of course, my amazing wife, Gabrielle.

Thanks also, to all of the amazing people who helped and hosted me on the journey.

Lastly, and especially, Bob Prior, who saved my life. More than once.

LIST OF ILLUSTRATIONS

Mongolia. The goal achieved!

Mongolia. The family; sweet helpful people.

Mongolia. Mother simmers testicular plov on a dung fired stove

Barnaul, Siberia. Never did discover why they buried the bikes in sand.

Kazakhstan. The Bong. Not really to my taste.

Kazakhstan. The Bong II Chrome helmet, presented by ex-Spetnatz.

Kazakhstan. The Refinery Hotel.

Kazakhstan. My first meeting with Mr. Paul A. Smith.

Kazakhstan. The Buran begins.

Kazakhstan. The Surgeon. "No cure for broken bones. Party on."

Saratov, Russia. Village Road.

Saratov, Russia. Occupied village house.

Saratov, Russia. The yard in a village house.

Saratov, Russia. Famous for three seconds.

Russian Ukrainian border. It's good be to back.

Kyiv, Ukraine. The Inner Sea, a huge hydro power station.

Proper navigation tools.

FURTHER READING

Signed copies of the first book in the series, Notes from the Road Vol IV. are available from the author at **www.derekmansfield.com**

To make direct contact write to **derek @derekmansfield.com**

Facebook **https://www.facebook.com/derek.mansfield.37**

Or Google Derek Mansfield.

YOUR JOURNEY STARTS HERE...